VIOLIN TIME

'There is nobody else like him' *Independent on Sunday*

'I don't think there is a more hilariously anarchic talent on the loose in British theatre' *The Times*

'The high-priest of storytelling theatre' *Time Out*

'The first quantum stage performer' *Evening Standard*

'The master of baroque banter – of vorticist structures that bind thought and anecdote together into surprisingly logical illustrations of the lunacy of existence' *Guardian*

'The only time I feel like dusting down the term ''genius'', in the pure sense of an influential demonic character, is when I'm confronted by a great Campbell show' *Observer*

'It is no accident he went to school in Barking. His contribution to British theatre is radical and immense' *Financial Times*

Ken Campbell founded the Science Fiction Theatre of Liverpool in 1976 where he directed two monumental epics: the twenty-two hour cult show *The Warp*, and *Illuminatus!* which was chosen to open the Cottesloe at the National Theatre in London. He also founded the legendary *Ken Campbell's Roadshow*. He is the author of the children's plays *Old King Cole*, *Skungpoomery*, *School for Clowns*, *Clowns on a School Outing*, *Peef* and *Frank 'n' Stein*, plus books for two musicals: *Bendigo* and *Walking Like Geoffrey*. His film scripts have included *Unfair Exchanges*, which starred Julie Walters, and *The Madness Museum*. On television he played Fred Johnson, Alf Garnett's neighbour in *In Sickness and in Health*. Ken Campbell's three semi-autobiographical shows, *Furtive Nudist*, *Pigspurt* and *Jamais Vu* (winner of the 1993 *Evening Standard* Best Comedy award), were performed at the Royal National Theatre as *The Bald Trilogy* in 1993. In 1994 he performed *Mystery Bruises (The Quantum Mechanical Humour Show)* at the Almeida Theatre, London. He has also made two 3-part programmes for Channel 4, interviewing scientists (*Reality on the Rocks*) and philosophers.

by the same author

THE BALD TRILOGY
(The Recollections of a Furtive Nudist, Pigspurt, Jamais Vu)

SKUNGPOOMERY

with F.K. Waechter

CLOWN PLAYS
(School for Clowns, Clowns on a School Outing, Peef)

Ken Campbell

VIOLIN TIME

– *or The Lady from Montségur*

Methuen Drama

First published in Great Britain 1996
by Methuen Drama
an imprint of Reed International Books Ltd
Michelin House, 81 Fulham Road, London SW3 6RB
and Auckland, Melbourne, Singapore and Toronto
and distributed in the United States of America by
Heinemann, a division of Reed Elsevier Inc.,
361 Hanover Street, Portsmouth, New Hampshire NH 03801 3959

A CIP catalogue record for this book
is available at the British Library

ISBN 0 413 70960 4

Typeset by Wilmaset Ltd, Birkenhead, Wirral
Printed in Great Britain by
Cox & Wyman Ltd, Reading, Berkshire

To Ion Alexis Will
with grateful thanks
for all the security leaks over many years now

This version is what I hope I would be saying were *Violin Time* to be opening at the Cottesloe, Royal National Theatre tonight – but it's not 'til late September – four to five months away – and who can predict which shit hath hit what fan 'twixt now and then . . . ?

KEN CAMPBELL
6 May 1996

I: *The Lungs of the Building*

In which we learn that it is possible to have a SELF, but astoundingly difficult to acquire one

The Church, Gants Hill —
One Sunday morning, 1949 – and I had a cold —
As a Cub of Sixer material, I would have marched there to
    drum and bugle —
I don't remember what was being said, but I do remember my
    thought:
'This is the collapse of reason' —
and a door opened (in my mind) and there was the nodding
    man with the teeth —
implying jovial agreement —
his arms crossed —
I was in a shack or shed, and he in the doorway —
Through the door I could see the ocean —
and the vision remained while a massive iceberg moved
    slowly past —
And he is still nodding, as if waiting for me to notice
    something —
I noted he wore medieval underwear . . .
Then I focused on the left hand of his crossed arms —
He was subtly doing VERY ODD AND ALARMING
    THINGS WITH HIS INDEX FINGER —
The vision faded —
and my cold had gone.

There's a new café opening soon downtown St Johns,
    Newfoundland —
off Duckworth, near the Ship Inn —

Oriental cuisine (some of it unusual) —
often live music (check) —
A jokey Jolly Roger flag flies above the entrance —
Mrs Darlington, the proprietress, also teaches violin.

I've just done a three-episode series for Channel 4 —
I interviewed Philosophers here and in the States —
Philosophers are interested in the SELF . . .
Where do you see me? —
Yes, yes, I'm on the stage —
But where do YOU see me? —
In your eyes? —
Really? —
You see me with your eyes, but then that's relayed where? —
Inside your head – okay – onto what? —
A screen? —
And who's watching the screen? —
Is that YOU? – Is that your SELF? —
But then the chaps who get paid to ponder these things say:
that geezer watching the screen must have another little geezer
     inside him who's watching another (titchy) screen, and
     there must be another geezer inside that, etcetera – which
     would be ridiculous . . .
And anyway, brainial surgeons can't find that bit —
They can take the top of your head off and ping a bit here and
     your left leg goes up —
or they can ping this bit there and you're talking about your
     Granny —
But they can't find any YOU —
any SELF —
Princess Di's had a go, and even she couldn't —
It's a thing we need, the SELF —
a thing we think must be there —
but a thing we haven't yet found.

Oxford Philosophers get in a lather about Artificial
  Consciousness:
'Yes,' they say, 'they can build a machine that can beat you at
  chess —
BUT DOES IT KNOW IT'S WON? —
Even if a light comes on and the thing waves a flag —
it still doesn't know it's won —
Not with the same flavour —
not with the same what-it's-likeness —
the same QUALIA that YOU get when you win' —
I said: 'Just 'cos you can't find the SELF doesn't mean it isn't
  there —
it could just mean it's good at hiding . . .
and if, say, it's the size of a few neuronal cells and the SELF
  inside that is, I dunno, atom-size, and the one inside that is
  quark-size —
and CERN is now telling us quarks aren't elemental —
so inside that it's the size of a Spook Quark . . .
One's SELF is like a funnel maybe —
and maybe due to our diet and life-style we've all got Spook
  Quarks clogging up our funnels, and if we could blow 'em
  through *kerphoom!* we'd make contact with the Archon
  Domain of Eternal Incredible Laughter . . . ?' —
Galen Strawson said: 'Possible. Of course. But it's not the
  thinking' —
Richard Dawkins said crack-pot speculation wasn't his area.

The last interview was to be the Star Interview —
with Derek Parfit —
Parfit's a Fellow of Old Souls, Oxford —
And Young Glover, son of Old Glover, told me this:
that for fourteen years Parfit clocked in —
always on time —
went up to his room and sat —
It was supposed he was thinking —
And then small minds made it a scandal —

'Should that Parfit chap *do* something? – I don't know . . .
   meet a student . . . ? Give a lecture . . . ?' —
Someone was dispatched to convey the feeling —
'O Lord,' said Parfit . . . 'Shall I write a book?' —
Fine! —
Derek's writing a book! —
and a year later he had it done: *Reasons and Persons*[1] —
and this puts Parfit up there with (most say above)
   Heidegger —
Kant —
Descartes —
and Plato —
Reasons and Persons —
a long work of such intricate philosophical complexity it will
   take the next two hundred years to digest it —
I was given a week off to read it before the interview.

My fave Philosopher is a kind of Anti-Philosopher: Marvin
   Minsky —
Minsky founded the Department of Artificial Intelligence at
   MIT Boston —
The interview took place in his house —
and his house . . . is awesome . . . astounding . . .
It's a big house, but you can hardly get through it —
Has he *ever* thrown anything away? —
It's like going back in time before the invention of the bin —
Everything of the Minsky life is coming at you from the walls
   and down from the ceiling —
If you take your hat off and put it down, you can't see it! —
It's ALL there —
Weird gadgets and wotnot, but also down to some toffee paper
   his kid had forty years ago —
'You're just a suitcase,' said Minsky —
'Whatever happens to be on top, that's your consciousness —
But everything underneath, that's you too' —
(His is the suitcase that exploded) —

'The SELF is an illusion —
There's no problem with Artificial Consciousness —
*we can build a thing that thinks it's got something it
    hasn't!* —
Everything that goes on in you breaks down to something very
    simple —
but there are several billion trillion very simple things,
and we haven't got them all mapped yet – ' —
I said: 'I've met some people who'd disagree with you' —
He said: 'Would these be people from Oxford, England?' —
I said yes —
He said: 'Oxford had some great minds —
Sadly they haven't had a new thought since 1750 —
Now they're on John Searle's QUALIA bandwagon —
If you hear a guy say QUALIA, you know you're talking to a
    very lazy person —
they just say QUALIA and collect the check – ' —
Minsky's terrific —
if he's wrong, he's the right kind of wrong: —
he wears a fishing jacket and only reads Science Fiction —
'I don't get it with regular literature —
It's been going on for thousands of years —
and it's just people coming in and out of doors —
sometimes they go some place —
fall in love – kill someone —
It's a very narrow spectrum —
but Science Fiction is about EVERYTHING ELSE.'

Minsky on religion:
'Religion has a use —
Some guy'll come up to you and say, "Is there a God?" —
and maybe you say, "Yeah, there's a God" —
and then he says: "So who made God?" —
and that's what Religion's for —
It looks after the Fruitless Reason Loops —
while we get on with things – ' —

And Minsky's got on with things —
REALLY GOT ON WITH THINGS.

Years ago: 1971 —
There was a season of lectures devoted to the weird and
   abstruse,
held (curiously) at the Victoria Palace —
One night we had Cleve Backster —
Backster was an inventor of ever-smarter lie detectors —
American —
He was a busy kind of guy, he told us —
and one coffee break, he was in the Reception Area and
   noticed that they'd moved in a rubber plant —
And he thought: 'I wonder if I'll get a reading?' —
and he plugged up the rubber plant to a lie detector —
and yeah! he got a reading —
and he thought, 'Hey, what happens if I TORTURE it??!' —
and he borrowed a cigarette and plunged it into the rubber
   plant —
and yeah! he got a reaction —
But then he noticed he'd got an even bigger reaction from the
   thing AT THE MOMENT WHEN HE'D THOUGHT:
   'WHAT HAPPENS IF I TORTURE IT?'!!! —
And he thought: 'Hey, what gives with PLANTS?!' —
and he packed his office with plant life and plugged it all up to
   lie detectors —
and he became of the opinion that his plants knew about
   HIM! —
wherever he was! —
He had to fly a lot, selling his new improved lie detectors to
   different Cop Authorities —
and he's a nervous flier, he's telling us —
when a plane takes off he gets a rush of shit to the heart —
same when it lands —
and you never know the EXACT moment when a plane's
   going to take off / land —

and he took to taking the time of those EXACT moments —

and when he'd get back to his office he'd see from the
   printouts that his plants had all known that something was
   up with their Cleve —   .

His experiences were written up in a book called *The Secret
   Life of Plants*[2] —

And I heard from seekers who claimed to have taken him out
   for a drink afterwards that one time there'd been a
   particularly gory murder in a greenhouse in Chicago and
   Backster had persuaded the cops to plug up all the plants to
   lie detectors, round up all the usual suspects and have them
   parade through the greenhouse —

AND IT WAS CLEAR WHO'D DUNNIT! —

And so the cops fitted him up, and he's still doing time —

(Even today, in an American Court of Law, it is still
   inadmissible,

the testimony of tomatoes —

Which is a shame —

the O.J. Simpson business could have been over in an
   afternoon if they'd plugged into the azaleas by the
   steps . . .) —

And for years I've been wondering when someone (apart from
   the Heir to the Throne) is going to take a proper interest in
   these matters —

and this year I found the folk who are:

They're an artists' commune who call themselves the Nation
   of Damanhur[3] —

they plug up trees through synthesisers and wotnot and you
   hear

the music of the trees —

and Charles is right —

they do respond to our music, and if you play at them they
   change their tune —

and you can buy these Spiraglic Thingies at Damanhur with
   which you can communicate with plants —

Interestingly they're called SELFS —
and they can do all sorts of things, these SELFS —
This one costs a lot because it's got lots of Spiraglia in there at
   the bottom
which you can't see or get at —
(that's ALCHEMICAL water in there) —

So there I was up in the Italian Alps having my first
   conversation with a tree the week I was meant to be reading
   Derek Parfit's book . . .
How had this happened?

Norman had moved in and he was excited that quite a lump of
   Violin Time was going to be about the Cathar heretics, and
   he was adamant (for reasons which will later be obvious)
   that that bit be spot on —
And he was insistent that we should visit the sites of alleged
   Neo-Catharism[4] or Pseudo-Catharism in the Alps if for no
   other reason than to check out Gillian's claim that it all had
   to do with CERN —
It would also be an opportunity for me to check out Norman's
   credentials.

Neo/Pseudo(?)-Cathars —
October '94: —
Dr Luc Jouret and Jo di Mambro herd their mainly French-
   Canadian flock out of Montreal and to the Swiss Alps for
   what the *Sunday Times* will call 'ALPINE
   ARMAGEDDON' —
In Cheiry, the House of Twenty-Three – i.e. twenty-three folk
   (kids included) will burn themselves up:
binbags of petrol taped to a timed electric cooker —
a ritual exit – robes, and in a circle —
looks of sublime happiness reported on many of the faces —

farewell jokey letters having been sent out signed 'D. Part'
   and wotnot —
and a few hours later, Salvan – the House of Twenty-Five –
   similar —
That burn-up will include Jouret and di Mambro[5] —
Who says they were Cathars? The CIC —
Ian Howarth of the Cult Information Centre tells me that di
   Mambro thought himself to be the reincarnation of Keeper
   of Cathar Secrets, Knight Templar,[6] Jacques de Molay —
When the Inquisition slow-roasted Jacques he was one of
   fifty-four consumed by Righteous Flame —
and if you add the Cheiry twenty-three to the Salvan twenty-
   five, plus the Canadian five a few days earlier, you get
   fifty-three – one short of the goal due to Thierry Huguenin
   who unofficially D. Camped before the official D. Part
   and wrote a book on it all called:
Le 54e[7] —
And the *Sunday Times*[8] says they were Cathars —
But they don't tell you what Cathars are —
they assume you know —
Actually, *they're not allowed to tell you* —
because if they did, all their readers'd go 'O yes of course' and
   never bother buying the *Sunday Times* again —
(and don't look smug Michael,[9] because I don't mean
   they'd switch to the *Observer* either) —
You can buy books on the Cathars, but they don't REALLY
   tell you —
There used to be books that REALLY told you, but they've
   all been burned —
There used to be people that REALLY told you, but they've
   all been burned —
well —
not quite all —
because there's one they didn't burn standing before you
   now —
and REALLY tell you is what he proposes now to do . . .

You date Catharism by when you got rid of it —
'Eradicated 1244
With the fall of Montségur' —
It began acres before Jesus under other names —
In fact Jesus was one of them —
In fact Jesus was several of them —
Cathars believed that you shouldn't believe —
(They were Gnostics, and Gnostics only gnow what they
    gnow) —
and one of the things that was gperfectly obvious was that the
    Creator is a Mad Barmy Evil Deranged Demi-Urge[10] —
and all matter is evil down to the last atom and quark of the
    stuff —
The explanation of laughter and happiness is that it is a benign
    immateriality piercing in from the True God Almighty: the
    Nothing —
and this is not The Nothing Which Does Exist —
we speak here of The Nothing That Doth Not Exist —
The 'Gnothing' —
also known as the 'Archon Domain of Eternal Incredible
    Laughter' —
So not for them cold churches and vicars —
but firesides and dancing girls and comedians —
and although they believed that you shouldn't believe,
they supposed that you should suppose —
to the hilt —
to the end of the line —
endstation: mass hysteria —
only then might you blow through and blast out the spook
    quarks which clog your funnels, and for a short period let in
    some of Gnod Almighty Gnothing's Eternal Incredible
    Laughter.

Rabelais, whose compendiums of philosophic filth still stand
    knee and bollocks above all the rest, is in fact presenting us
    with CLEANED-UP Cathar tales[11] —

'To hoot at fate through life's short span
Is the proper course for Man' —
History is dated by extraordinary bouts of hilarity and
    legendary carousings —
Never by battles —
In Cathar stories, the only heroes are Comic Heroes, from
    wherever, whenever in history they are taken —

Rabelais again: 'Body: ugly; demeanour: ridiculous; stare of a
    cow; but always drinking with everyone, and always
    sharing that with which he brimmed, his laughter, his arsing
    about, his divine wisdom' is how Rabelais introduces
    Socrates into his narrative —
SEEKER'S VOICE: 'But aren't we talking Troubadour and
    Minstrel, and didn't they sing awful tragic mournful stuff?
    That's what I was taught . . .' —
ME: 'Yes, you probably were, but that's 'cos them 'at taught
    you taught you wrong —
It'd be like being four hours with Ken Dodd and then reporting
    he sang "Tears My Souvenirs" – all you was taught about
    was the tail-end ditties – the closers' —
The Inquisition WON! —
You were taught by the descendants of the Inquisition! —
The first job of the seeker on leaving school is to UNlearn —
Otherwise you'll never gnow Gnothing.
Haphazard, I open my *Burlesque et obscénité chez les
    troubadours*[12] at . . .
'The Song of the Fotedor' —
in the original OC —
This stuff comes from the bit of France that can't stand the
    French —
The Languedoc – Langue d'OC – where they don't say 'Oui'
    for 'yes' but 'OC':[13]
*'Lo FOTaire es tant de FOTre angoissos,
Com plus fort FOT, mor FOTant de felnia*

*Que plus non FOT, qu'el FOTria per dos
De FOTedors melhors de Lombardia – ' —*

In the modern French notes they translate FOT with
    '*baiser*' —
baiser being the French for 'fuck' – but kinda milder – *baiser*
    can be used in conversation with most grannies these
    days —
But ask any OC speaker – this misses it, Pierre —
FOT means 'to fuck uncaring of which orifice'[14] —
Toreadors, picadors, matadors . . .
But the guy who really puts the breeze up the bulls is the
    fotedor.

Montségur —
The last two hundred-plus Cathars under siege, way up, on the
    high little fortress —
they hold out eight months —
they run out of water —
they ask for a truce of two weeks, then they'll simply come
    down and offer themselves to the flames —
Agreed —
They came down —
like a carnival —
many with the cut 'onky' ('*homme qui rit*')[15] mouth of their
    comic hero
Norman 'Le Croc' de Dijon —
capering —
singing 'The Song of the Fotedor' —
they jumped into the fires —
AND LAUGHED FROM THE BLAZE —
It was always Cathar's Honour to laugh from the flames —
'cos it really freaks 'em! —
and it demonstrates with your last uttering that you've made it
    to the True God:

The Gnothing: The Archon Domain of Eternal Incredible
    Laughter —
and there's a trick to it: —
to be burned alive is very painful —
for the first bit —
But soon it burns away all feeling —
and then what you are is COOL —
Hang on – hang on for that bit —
and then hahahaHAR 'Aceeedio!' with your last.

Jacques de Molay was a bit later —
By the time they got to him, they were wise to it —
to cut down on the cackling they slow-roasted him —
but even so, he still managed two chuckles from the spit for
    which in some circles he is still revered.

Rabelais would have known his SETH, but he left out
    SETH —
(the fires of the Inquisition still burned as he progressed his
    extraordinary project) —
The Cathars, whom some authorities call a Christian sect, had
    their own Gospels —
Their Jesus didn't DIE for us – he arsed around for us —
(some dispute that it was actually 'for us') —
THE SECOND TREATISE OF THE GREAT SETH[16] is
    available through your library
(although ordering it may get you put on a list . . .) —
SETH is a comedy monologue by our Lord, and the Great Seth
    some kind of Michael Billington of the day, when evidently
    it was the form to try and jot down the whole routine —
I quote the scholarly Intro:
'The God of this world is evil and ignorant . . . his minions
    counterfeits and laughing-stocks . . . the crucifixion is that
    of the Gnostic Basilides . . . Simon of Cyrene is crucified in
    place of the laughing Jesus' —
The crucifixion bit of the rap goes like this:

In Cyrene (a kind of Romford district of Palestine) was, at the
time shit was about to hit the fan, one Simon —

From one side, if you only looked quick, he bore a passing
resemblance to our Lord, and he approached Him with his
idea:

'Lord, Lord – ' said Simon, 'I'm just a nerd really – nothing
much going for me at all (I come from Cyrene!) – whereas
you, if half what they're saying is true . . .

Wouldn't it be better if they crucified ME!' —

And Jesus saw the Wisdom of this —

and so it went —

Jesus was half a mile away up a hill when they crucified
Simon —

and He reports that when He saw that absolutely everyone had
been taken in —

He just couldn't help laughing.

Common herbert Cathar tradition has it that after that He and
Mary Magdalene took off and settled in France where their
kids became the Holy Royal line of Kings – Dagobert the
this and that – the Merovingian Dynasty —

(That Royal Holy bloodline comes into our own Royal Family
at Henry VI and VIII and dangadangadang down, unbroken,
to our own Queen and Prince Philip, who are BOTH direct
descendants from the loins of Queen Victoria, but not first
cousins, so their children shouldn't be potty) —

These were all things known to Jean Cocteau —

1900s-ish the Vicar of Rennes-le-Château dug up papers
proving the Holy Line from all the kids Jesus had had after
his crucifiction, blackmailed the Vatican, and died a
millionaire having converted his church into a marvellously
garish Romperama, and devoted his life to annoying his
flock and arsing about with tarty opera singers —

A fine comic[17] can be purchased in the bookshop at
Montségur for the seeker requiring fuller detail.

But Jean Cocteau also knew this:

Jesus wasn't just one geezer —
SETH again:
JESUS: 'I visited a bodily dwelling. I cast out the one who was
    in it first, and then I went in' —
Do you get it? —
He wasn't actually a geezer at all because geezers are made of
    matter —
He was a bit of benign immateriality which bobbed from one
    to another —
JESUS WAS THE NAME FOR THE GUY WITH THE BEST
    JOKES THAT NIGHT —
and you can crucify the bloke, but you can't crucify the
    joke! —
(not if it's a goodun) —

Gnosis magazine[18] —
front cover reproducing a goings-on in a thirteenth-century
    church —
early 1200s, and Dominico Guzman, representing the Pope, is
    holding debates with the Cathars —
Anciente pic shows Guzman putting Cathar books on a little
    fire he's made in the church —
Now those books are going to blaze away no problem —
but then he's going to put a Holy Bible onto the flames, and
    not only will that not burn, it's going to pang out of the fire
    with such force, such velocity, it will both singe and bruise
    the beam —
Sadly that little church has now burned down —
but the Dominican monks still have the beam —
and if you call on 'em they're delighted to tell you the tale —
But you have to go down to the pub and take aside an OC
    speaker to hear the Cathar reply to this stunt:
Troubadour/Minstrel (which means he made up his own
    material) Norman 'Le Croc' de Dijon (day job: undertaker!)
    was taking on Dominico that day —
And the great 'Le Croc' —

(ripped comedy mouth of the 'onky' —
picture a cross between Errol Flynn and Bernard Manning –)
was put in to bat for the Cathars —
AND HE TURNED WATER INTO WINE! —
He did it with dodgy mushrooms and veg dye —
The official definition of wine then was 'red and gets you
   pissed' —
and this was a corker —
some died! —
and then the conjuring bout over —
and clearly a win to the Cathars when Dominico's crude
   panger was uncovered —
The Great Debate began . . .

NORMAN: Is God male?
DOMINICO: Yes.
NORMAN: So He's got a dick?
DOMINICO: No.
NORMAN: So how we know He's a man?
DOMINICO: He's got a – but He . . . calls it a penis.
NORMAN: Who's He FOT with it?
DOMINICO: He doesn't FOT.
NORMAN: Just uses it to pee?
DOMINICO: He doesn't pee.
NORMAN: So why's He got it?
DOMINICO: He just thought it would be nice to have one.

This brought the house down, and we're now approaching the
   major turning point of Western Civilisation —
this debate had now given Dominico a role —
Norman's stooge —
Known now as Dominico 'Just Thought It Would Be Nice To
   Have One' Guzman, he was laughed at, yes, but he'd
   become, in a sense, popular —
and Norman offered him a partnership —
The Laurel to his Hardy —

the Thin One of Abbott and Costello to his Fat One —
and these debates had commercial potential —
and the Troubadour Touring Circuit VAST —
it's on page 80 of *Atlas of the Crusades*![19] —
And which way Dominico will go will seal all our fates . . .
Mmmm!? —
He'd been to school, seekers —
but hadn't unlearned anything —
and he persuaded himself he was making the good and brave
   decision to forgo a beckoning showbiz career and skuttle
   back to the Pope —
(Pope Innocent III —
the form then to adopt a satirical name) —

INNOCENT: 'Just Thought It Would Be Nice To Have One',
   Dominico . . . ?
DOMINICO: Yes. There's naught to be done with 'em, sire, by
   debate. I think we'll have to burn them . . .
INNOCENT: I'd like you to meet Simon de Montfort. He's
   wonderful. No sense of humour whatsoever —

(Béziers . . . Flames and Laughter —
Carcasonne . . . A Chuckling Furnace —
Toulouse . . . Barbecue of Hootings and Acedios) —

'But sire, many here be not comedians!' —
DE MONTFORT: 'Burn them all. The Lord will know his
   own' —

(Minerve . . . some cinders —
Montségur. All gone. Everything. —
And yet) —

Dominico Guzman we now know as St Dominic —
We name colleges of learning and essay prizes after de
   Montfort —
(I've never read any of his essays —
are they any good?) —

And ever after wert our funnels clogged.

So Jouret and di Mambro and Salvan and Cheiry —
(But we never heard of Cathars setting light to
    themselves . . .) —
And then just before Christmas 1995 the 'Vercours-near-
    Grenobles Sixteen' —
Mambro and Jouret's Solar Templars, the Sixteen's farewells
    claimed —
including wife and son of Olympic ski champ —
A woodland glade the setting for this mass combustion —
Pissed off they'd not been invited on the big 'un just over a
    year before. . . ? —
(*but might not they be a rival troupe hoping to severely mucks-
    up the numbering?*) —
And the ALPS . . . Shouldn't it be the Pyrénées? —
Why the wrong mountain range? —
'Cos they're Canadians. . . ? —
And then Moirans[20] —
Moirans, little town in French Alps —

THINGS combusting there[21] —
a tin of oranges in a drawer suddenly combusts with pongy
    blue flame —
sack of cement! – same pongy blue flame —
Then a couple of human self-combustions in Moirans —
you know, where your pants are kind of all right, but you're
    not —
Salvan, Cheiry, Grenobles, Moirans – none far from each
    other . . .
And always the big question:
Couldn't they have found somewhere nice to set light to
    themselves in Montreal? —
Especially when the last straw for the cult seems to have been
    their treatment by the Hydro-Quebec Electric
    Company?! —

Gillian (who is not on all subjects sound, I've come to realise)
   had said: 'CERN' —
And it had made sense.

CERN —
I know about CERN because I had to interview folk there for a
   Channel 4 Science series[22] —
CERN is the most expensive Scientific Experiment ever
   undertaken by Man —
CERN is so big it's the name of the place —
CERN is two-thirds in France and one-third in Switzerland —
The main biz is underground, and what it is is a 27km tube
   containing nothing —
And by nothing I don't mean 'not awfully much really' —
not a vacuum – there's loads of crap in vacuums —
this is real nothing —
nigh on the Nothing That Doesn't Exist is what they've got in
   there —
There is more NOTHING in that 27km sausage THAN
   ANYWHERE ELSE IN THE KNOWN UNIVERSE —
Space is teeming with stuff compared to what they haven't got
   in the CERN tube —
and what they do with it is wazz round subatomic particles
at the speed (almost) of light —
they collide, and new matter is formed —
the particles don't mutate —
they're a bit dazed but OK —
but out of the energy of the wazzing (or some not yet
   understood quality in the NOTHING) new matter is
   formed —
They've been doing this for seventeen years or so now, and I'd
   assumed they'd be able to show us at least half a jam jar of
   it —
but sadly, no —
what we're talking about is very small indeed —
and it only lasts for a few instants of Time —

and you wouldn't have known it was there at all if you hadn't
   bothered to build yourself a computer rather larger than
   Westminster Abbey —
And it's got enormous cabling round it —
It looks like several Pompidou Centres – (all there underground!) —
I asked if it had to be that big because they were using old-
   fashioned technology and they said No, everything here,
   man, is right up to the Mark^{23} —
and they grin – they all grin – they love it there —
they come from all over the world to wazz, and they love it —

Anyway, in a small way they're duplicating the Big Bang
   when the fault ('error', Sadie calls it) occurred in the Grand
   Celestial Buggerall —
I said, 'Is there any chance you're going to set off another
   Universe inside ours?'
and the older Czech scientist, who chainsmokes cigarillos,
   gave an 'Uncly' dismissive laugh like you used to hear in
   Episode Ones of *Quatermass* serials —
Signor Amaldi, who was Head of Wazzing at the time, said
   that 'For many of us here at CERN, the interest is no longer
   the wazzing of particles BUT THE NOTHING IN THE
   TUBE' . . .

You get it? —
To the Cathar, a 27km sos of nothing is a 27km sos of Heaving
   Divine Jollity —
Hence probably the CERN grin —
a leakage of the ABSOLUTE —
'Outbreak of God in Area 9!' —
But more to the point, hence the attraction of that part of the
   world to the Canadian Combusters —
(it made immediate sense to me soon as Gillian said CERN —
I got it —
(and radiated)) —

Because it would aid them in their REINCARNATIVE
  intent —
('Transit to Sirius' we take to be code) —
To depart from current body and D. Part to another's —
'I visited a bodily dwelling.
I cast out the one who was in it first, and I went in' –
  Jesus[24] —
In one of the latest two of David Icke's books, I think (and I'd
  check it out for you if some Dick hadn't gone off with
  both), he tells us that Justinian removed all the remaining
  references to reincarnation from the Official Bible in (?)
  500 A.D. (can you bring those books back please, Seeker,
  because, as you see, I DO need them and actually they're
  terrific) —
Anyway, why would he remove that stuff? —
Because it *didn't* work? —
Nah! So's he and his brood'd be the only ones who gnew and
  had the gnowhow,
and put any who stumbled on the Secret in bins! —

Anyway, with the extra ooompf shooting up the Alps from the
  CERN Hilarity Tube, they could reincarnate in/possess/
  par-possess key living individuals in the Pyramid of
  Power[25] readying us for the Joy of Overt Cathar Takeover
  scheduled for the beginning of the next millennium —
If the Solar Templars are wrong, they're tragic possibly, stupid
  certainly —
If they're right – *we are* —
They went to the end of the line . . .
AND THEN DREW IT! —

Cathars gnew about reincarnation —
they investigated it fully and practised it —
You can: —
When your next child is born, keep it in the dark, literally —
Let him/her know only firelight —

let you teach it to speak without once it having looked in a
  mirror —
It mustn't start taking an interest in who it IS until we've
  found out who it WAS! —
(and the joyful cry would come up from the Cathar fireside:
  'Roger's back!') —
Also do this: —
Secretly, known only to yourself (NO WRITTEN
  RECORD!) —
bury some bizarre and singular item —
to be your reincarnative CREDENTIAL in some future
  century.

So yes, we go check out these sites, Norman —
(and the CERN connection –) —
But the only week I could go was the week off I'd been given
  to read Parfit —
I said, 'I can't go Norman —
I've got to read all about Is the Self Self-Determining?; Self-
  Interests of a Reverse Self; Shelf Life of the Self's Life;
  What the Self Did Next; Self on a Treasure Island and
  stuff' —
Idly we had typed SELF into the InterNet Search and it came
  up with Damanhur —
where they make and market SELFS (?) —
and not only that, they'd hollowed out the inside of a mountain
  with buckets and built the Tempio dell'Uomo in it as an
  investigation into the SELF[26] —
in the Italian ALPS . . .
and also roughly equidistant from CERN . . .
Oh! – I dunno – yeah – no —
And I was distracting myself with junk mail and came across
  this: from 'Life Tools. PhotoReading – Blast through books
  at 25,000 words a minute . . . Not Speed-reading . . . a new
  technique . . .'[27] —
I rang 'em up —

Two hundred quid and a bit more to rush me one —
and these cassettes and books is it[28] —
'Yeah, let's go, Norman – this obviously works – I'll do the
    course on the way from ghoulish site to ghoulish site, and
    I'll blast through Parfit when we get back, just in time for
    the Interview!' —

The trick is to lodge the target book in your UNconscious
    mind and then develop the knack of accessing only the bits
    you need —
There's room for whole libraries in there! —
In fact it's not really 'reading' at all, it's a whole other biz —
First you've got to find your Phantom Sausage —
Everyone's got one —
Or everyone with two eyes has —
(If you've only got one eye you do something else –) —
Do it now! —
Wave your arms about —
Come on – (ETC.) —
Good, that's just so there's no embarrassment when we come
    to what you have to do —
Look at something distant and static —
So not at me —
Something on the stage —
Now in front of your eyes bring your two index fingers
    together while keeping focused distant —
and you'll see it! – You'll see your sausage! —
(It's due to the Divergence of Vision) —
You can make it dance! —
Mine's dancing! —
Make your sausage dance! —
A dancing sausage look! —
And that's how you do it —
You look past the book over the top of it and in the middle a
    phantom sausage page appears and that's all you bother
    with —

Soon as you got it you turn the page —

Don't stop and READ anything or it will interrupt your lack of concentration.

There is of course more to it than that —

You have to practise page-turning —

Important to keep up a relentless rhythmic momentum —

Sos – Turn – Sos – Turn – Sos – Turn —

And you have to develop a tangerine on the top of your head —

An imaginary tangerine —

actually a few inches above your head —

(none of this was known to Jean Cocteau) —

(which was why he wrote short books) —

You have to be AWARE of your tangerine throughout the entire Bookblast —

In fact the sausage needs to feed straight through and into the tangerine —

To access your Blastings you then just gently squeeze your tangerine.

Terrific! —

I've in fact improved on the technique —

(I've written to them about it but I haven't had a reply yet) —

When we got back, here's what I did —

I made this out of a box [sort of cardboard TV thing] —

In the box I put this to focus on, and it is in fact the Italian magazine *Focus* open at the article[29] about how the Italians have found another brain – in the stomach – it operates your arsehole; arseholes have a mind of their own, literally (an idea I heard about three years ago from an incredibly attractive larger sort of girl in Newfoundland, of which more later) —

So I put this diagram of the Italian Arsehole Brain in the Box as my static concentration point —

To be viewed through this Alchemical Spiraglic —

Then —

(and this is the biggy) —

This is a perfectly ordinary sink plunger —

I remove the handle —
and replace it with this —
(I don't know if you can get these here —
it's an Alpine Honey Spoon) —
and then the spoon handle goes up a tangerine —
(orange for a heavier work) —
And [sink plunger on head]! —
I'd worked out that to Bookblast Parfit's *Reasons and Persons*
    would take $17\frac{1}{2}$ minutes —
And with this weight of orange, that's about what you can
    take —
which seems to me to be neater than what the course tells you
    to do:
Have a clock nearby to glance at —
(That surely buggers up your lack of concentration) —
Then, for good measure, into the orange I stuck the
    Damanhurian plant communication selficatious spiraglic.
How did the Interview go? —
Fine. One of the best —
Parfit is a charming man[30] —
And whenever it was needed, I simply squeezed my orange —
But I'd say this:
After the Interview, Derek Parfit looked ever so slightly pissed
    off that I knew so much.

CERN[31] —
of course, a sensation for me again, and Norman (first time) —
Apparently NOTHING is the big one now —
What are the mathematics of NOTHING? —
One NOTHING is NOTHING —
Two NOTHINGS are NOTHING of the same lack of size —
But Sadie's way ahead with how many Nothings That Don't
    Exist (what is the critical mass of them Non-Existent
    Nothings) before a catastrophe and *wallop!* you've got a
    Nothing Which Does Exist on your hands —

and how many of them buggers before Something
   happens? —
It gives a deep meaning to the hitherto throwaway phrase:
   Does it matter? —
The mighty magnets of CERN (each one heavier than the
   Eiffel Tower), which keep the Nothing from doing
   anything, are, in cross-section, eerily similar to the stained-
   glass Temple ceilings at Damanhur —
But hang on! —
After CERN was Salvan, then Cheiry: —
Breathtaking – very high in the Swiss Alps —
Jouret and di Mambro certainly hadn't chosen grubby
   locations for them and their flock's end —
('Have a good end' is the traditional goodbye of the
   Cathars) —
Grenobles: I lost my sausage for a worrying hour —
Moirans: lot of humour with two old ladies in the toy-shop
   (where I got the honey spoon) who'd known the self-
   combusters – knew the make of tin of the oranges – had a
   theory, and are coming to stay, for which I can thank
   Norman —
But why we'd gone turned out to be Damanhur . . .

On the drive to Damanhur (about an hour and a half after you
   get out of the Mont Blanc Tunnel) I'd put away the
   Bookblasting tapes, and Norman and I wrestled towards a
   Creed of Modern Catharism:

'There was the Gnothing and only the Gnothing a.k.a. The
   Archon Domain of Eternal Incredible Laughter —
it had the potential to create any kind of Universe, possible
   and impossible —
but the Grace, Mercy and Wisdom not to —
then this fault occurred (our Universe) —
(blame a Mad Barmy Evil Deranged Demi-Urge if you like —
but it could set you off on Fruitless Reason Loops) —

Smaller than a pinhead at first – in fact smaller, dimensionless,
   it got so hot and heavy that it *kaboomed* outwards[32] —
a dreadful crashing and banging of ever-expanding ice, fire
   and din —
Black Holes, Red Dwarfs (the news from the Hubble is
   increasingly bleak) —
Eternal Incredible interfered and managed, after a lot of arsing
   about,
to get us going —
We are his[33] peek into the awful mess —
Our job is to work out what it is and wind it up —
(while having as much fun as possible —
humour is our only direct line to the Divine) —
Left to itself it will expand on ludicrously and for the rest of
   forever, ultimately an eternal ice monument to its own
   foolishness —
Our job is to get the Universe sufficiently conscious to realise
   its own futility and have the wit to stop and go back,
   crunching and imploding back down to the singularity – and
   then if they're doing their job in the Laughter Zone they can
   stop it roaring back out the other side —
Why we can't namby about rooting for Qualias —
imperative we get conscious humour into the so-called
   inanimate —
Another notion is to eat away at the whole show from inside
   with fast-breeding double (triple?)[34] Light-Speed anti-
   matter universe —
The CERN experiments give us hope here —
but it's still a wild card, eschatologically speaking —
The Crunch idea has more obvious humour inherent in it,
   because once we reverse things Time'll go backwards —
you'll sit on the toilet and the poo'll go up your bum
and you'll cough up a banana.'

There's Damanhur, the Artists' Commune (stained glasswork;
  mosaic; sculpting and painting; Selficatious spiraglics,
  etc.) —
and then a mile or two up the mountain and then into the
  mountain through a shed door behind a humble artisan's
  cottage and you're into the Tempio dell'Uomo.

Norman and I had the honour to be shown round by Oberto
  Airaudi, the Governor, Prince, King and Genius of the
  Democratic Nation of Damanhur (vibrantly gorgeous
  Esperide[35] translating between us)

¡
†
§
†
ß
ç
\
\

¿
¿¿¿¡¡!!!???

In the Temple many thoughts came —
Like: I shall have to talk about this —
but how do you make awe amusing? —
What is the language of astoundment? —
Let me compare it to here: [the Cottesloe] —
The first hall is perhaps the size of this stage —
bigger —
and it is sealed; no doors, no openings – and it's Ancient
  Egyptian —
except it's modern Ancient Egyptian —
Maybe some of you can write Ancient Greek or Latin —
these guys have taught themselves *hieroglyphs* —
and it's funny —
you can tell it's witty —
and in fact, what it's saying is: 'This is only starters' . . .

If you press the Pharaoh's nose, the wall slides and you're in
    the labyrinth —
They sometimes call the office corridors here [at the National
    Theatre] 'the labyrinth' —
Sorry – grey corridors you get lost in do not a labyrinth
    make —
A true labyrinth, by its layout and dimensions (the fact you
    have to duck exactly here, crouch right there and NOT over
    there) and by its decoration,
will *speak* to you —
Getting lost is not the point —
you are entranced, enchanted, intriguingly mystified by
    everywhere you find yourself —
No panic to get out —
only fear lest it come to an end too soon —
(and it doesn't) —
What productions might have been mounted here if every inch
    of NT corridor was thought-provokingly humorous (instead
    of grey with posters)? —
And then into boggling wonder of hall after hall —
masterpieces of stained-glass and mosaic —
immense —
the whole thing in that mountain – dug out by hand —
no caves —
the innards carried out in BUCKETS, in secret, over fifteen
    years —
by the Secret Nine to begin with, rising by the fifteenth year to
    the Secret Ninety —
Then one greedy Dick . . .
he'd worked on the project for a few years, then left —
was short of money and blackmailed them for half a
    million —
'Half a million or I tell the world you're in here' —
and this at the time of WACO and the Solar Templars of close
    proximity —
and Oberto said, No, there's no half a million for you —

But it meant he had to announce himself —
divulge the mighty secret —

It's as big as the whole of the National Theatre in there —
Here there are three halls, there they have seven —
each with its own acoustic —
one for strings, another for the human voice, and so on —
each hall with its own fragrance —
each one startling and reviving —
monstrous, sumptuous, sexy, funny, profound —
the Water Hall, the Hall of Spheres, the Earth Hall, etc. —
each incredible stained-glass illuminated ceiling always
    having an unfinished small rough corner exposing
    mountain —
The Lungs of the National Theatre complex are in the
    basement
by the Olivier Drum Revolve —
(Socially the Lung Room is used by the NT acting companies
    – for petting and fotting during their thespian lulls – and is
    sometimes (illegally but understandably) locked for the
    private comforting a caring director will give to a worried
    ingénue — .
Also dope fumes disperse quickly and without trace) —
The NT Lungs consist of pneumatic controlled dumpers which
    contain electronic-to-pneumatic conversion valves; chiller
    coils (supplied from reciprocating chillers) balanced by
    dual-fuel gas-oil burners – a plant management system of
    network stand-alone out-stations —
This supplies you with the air you breathe here, and the
    temperature required for optimum attention to the dramatic
    fare —
Compare the Temple Lung Room which supplies Damanhur's
    intra-mountain palace with variously and specifically
    fragranced air AND MAINTAINS A DRYNESS WHICH

BAFFLES THE MILITARY, and which includes an enormous tonnage[36] of static yet living[37] brass, copper, silver and gold spiraglia, much of which I was shown.

And is this alchemical water in here? [the item I brought back] —

Why not? —

There's a fully functioning alchemical laboratory in the Temple —

and Oberto —

forty-four now —

I asked him: 'Presumably you would have preferred to have kept it secret?' —

'Of course,' he said. 'It's only one-tenth complete and we have been allowed to go no further for four years —

We had no planning permission —

but if we'd asked to do this, they would have said no —

One of the plans is to evict us and the town to have it as a tourist attraction – ' —

not said bitterly, WITH HUMOUR —

'Did you all laugh a lot at the end of the day?' I asked —

'We laughed at the beginning of the day and all through it and at the end of it and most often through the night – you'd wake and someone was laughing – '[38] —

Where did all the money come from? —

I don't know —

I didn't ask —

Oberto bats around the place in a titchy one-man helicopter — he goes shopping in it —

They are going through a series of appeals —

to hang on to it and continue —

The Damanhur Tempio dell'Uomo is a coming together of influences of the very most ancient, and some security leaks from the future —

(somewhere in there you touch a Pharaoh's something else and a wall turns into a staircase) —

plus a consummate knowledge of today —
and I thought, Well, yeah, if rich nations of the world all
    pitched in, you could make a 27km sausage of nothing —
More Nothing than anywhere else in the known Universe —
and I'm not belittling that achievement —
but nine, rising ninety, men and women, in secret have done
    something else —
they've created more Something than anywhere else in the
    known Universe —
and I realised that I loved Oberto and I knew why —
He had a SELF —
all this doris-ing about: 'We think we have a SELF, it seems
    we have, to us, but have we? Qualia bollocks' is chat about
    the SEATING ARRANGEMENT —
we've got the seat for a SELF but no one sitting on it —
To get a SELF you have to ASTOUND it into being —
I understood now how the project was seen as an investigation
    into the Self —
They had astounded themselves by the day, by the minute with
    what they were capable of —
and Oberto certainly had a SELF —
and I thought, Maybe Minsky has too —
Minsky and Oberto both reeking of Qualia, and Minsky, by
    denying a Self exists and REALLY getting stuck into what
    you *can* do, has become the living antithesis of his
    stance —
He'd got one! —
Hahahaha! —
How funny —
Oberto and I laughed, but he didn't know why —
(actually he probably did) —

Oberto, who'd harvested the Fruitless Reason Loops! —
I'll tell you what it's like being with Oberto —
you know the piniony warmth of a pigeon's armpit? —
Like having your head up one —

You know he's seeing you, but he doesn't often look at you
    directly,
his visual periphery possibly the better to feed you into his
    unconscious —
sos you, and straight up into his tangerine —
and a tangerine he certainly has —
a whole bowl of fruit, I'd say —
I said: 'I suppose you can remember back through a lot of
    lives?' —
'Mmm,' he said. Later, and I can only suppose it was in
    answer to that question, he said: 'It would have been very
    difficult otherwise' —
And I thought some more about here [the National Theatre] —
after all, some months in the future I would, I suppose, be up
    here talking about these matters —
ROYAL National Theatre —
If it's ROYAL, shouldn't it have a pair of big fine ears
    sculpted and sticking proudly out from that thing?[39] —
and the outside decoration —
it's not as exciting as a New York subway train, is it? —
And what's NATIONAL about it? —
it's a production house —
so it does Shakespeare —
so this —
so that —
What's NATIONAL —
when was a Welsh choir? —
(Miners sing as well as strike don't they?) —
or anything IN Welsh? —
Surely in a NATIONAL theatre the NATION should SHOW
    us, not US show the Nation? —
at the very least, in here, the Cottesloe —
The first production ever in here was mine and Chris
    Langham's[40] —
It came from a derelict warehouse in Liverpool —
a big company we were, who had only done it for love of it —
we were so proud to be here —

and there was great hoo-hah about 'this was to be the shape of
   things' —
Was it? —
again? —
You with me? —
I don't mean great things weren't done in here —
You know what I mean —
Is there anything you could do now in a provincial warehouse
that would get you here? —
If the answer is 'no' it's quite simply a failure.
And so am I, I thought —
What happened? —

I always gnew you had to constantly astound yourself —
Is there time left for me to still astound up a SELF? —
'I'm not sure whether I could be with you if you had a SELF,'
   said Norman —
'Really? —
What did you make of Oberto?' —
'He's a Parfait, that for sure' —
Oberto was off to the shops in his helicopter —
'He has given me not doubts exactly . . .' —
(I assumed Norman was referring to our Creed of the Modern
   Cathar) —
'But an excitement of queries, certainly.'

That mountain site for the Temple wasn't chosen because it's
   only 20kms from the mountain up which they filmed *The
   Name of the Rose* —
(and that was filmed while the Temple was still all secret —
'Has Umberto Eco been here?' I'd asked —
'No,' said Oberto. 'Bring him.') —
But because it's on a telluric interchange —
the largest known conjunction of The Lines of Synchronos —
What they? —
Ley lines, song lines, dragon paths, I suppose —

Oberto has them all globally mapped[41] —
and also the site contains the greatest diversity of minerals
  planetwide —
(But presumably less now, after all the buckettings[42]) —
(Or maybe MORE now, with all the Spiraglia and stuff
  they've put in there!)

'Let's see where they filmed *The Name of the Rose*,' said
  Norman —
'I have a hunch there will be something for us there' —

Mrs Darlington's Musical Caff (it's in the harbour area across
  the water from where they dance so well) has one of its
  walls decorated in genuine Damanhurian spiraglic, and
  indeed the whole business is run on SELF-astoundment
  lines —
Mrs D writes every week to Oberto and Esperide and arranges
  visits to the Temple and Tree Concerts for Newfoundland
  seekers.

II: *Spiraglia*

In which the Lady from Montségur comes and goes; a military gentleman is rubbed by fine women; Cherokee terminology is etymologically examined; Newfoundland is visited and an early happy ending is scuppered by a violin; the question to which the answer will sometimes be 'coffee' is found in a field; and a Mystical Geography plan to cope with a young lady's sullen moods is proposed

Norman came into my life, breathless, August 28th, 1995, in
Montségur —
I was there on a particularly bizarre commission —
(which I will deal with, but later —
believe me, to go into the convolutions which had led me to be
  in that village, at that time, would ramificate and baffle
  beyond bearing —
It would have you all racing for the 'He goes' (my translation
  of 'EXIT') —
But later it will fit into place, snug —
Let's go now for the well-greased narrative —
the easier, if the Good Gnothing pleases, to astound) —

So —
Montségur, Aug. 27, 1995, and I was eating, alone, at this
  terrific little half-outdoor restaurant, cut into the foot of the
  mountain, at the very outskirts of the village —
It's above a little Bookshop, and the waiter there speaks very
  good English because he's worked in Australia —
'Where are you from?' he asked —
(This is the evening before Norman and I collide) —
I said from England, and he said: 'What, Bath?' —
'Bath?' I said, 'No, not Bath! Why *Bath*?' —
'O,' he said, and popped off down into the Bookshop and
  came back with this book: *Cathars and Reincarnation* by
  Arthur Guirdham[43] —

and Arthur was from Bath – he was a psychiatrist there
   twenty-five years ago —
and he had a patient – a lady patient —
and Arthur (who tells us he keeps an open mind on such
   matters)
thought it possible that she'd had a previous life —
Sometimes she'd wake up in the middle of the night with an
   urge to draw a very particular and curious kind of buckle –
   that sort of thing —
Arthur took a special interest and wrote off to various
   authorities and eventually became persuaded of the notion
   that she was some kind of reincarnated Cathar heretic from
   the Pyrénées region in the middle of the thirteenth
   century —
I mean, she was really coming out with knowledges that a
   simple Bath lady had no right to possess —
So Arthur said to Mrs Guirdham, 'You know, I think we ought
   to take my patient to the Pyrénées and see what
   happens.' . . .
Anyway, they went there, and it was so *moving* —
She knew where she was and what was round the corner! —
And then it turned out that Arthur himself had also been a
   Cathar in the thirteenth century —
and not only that, but he and his patient had been lovers all
   those years ago —
So they took to going there every summer after that —
(I don't think Mrs Guirdham went on all the trips) —

Arthur then brought out this moving book, *Cathars and
   Reincarnation*, as a result of which it transpired that there
   were eighteen or nineteen other good people of Bath, one of
   them a little kid, who were also reincarnated thirteenth-
   century Cathar heretics (a story Arthur tells us in his sequel,
   We Are One Another[44]) which was awfully handy, because
   it meant they could all go over together in a bus and get a
   much better rate on the ferry.[45] —

(I did a try-out of this show in Bath, and this guy came up
    afterwards who was a son of one of these reincarnateds,
    'dragged over there every year, me and my sister', and he
    now runs a Cycling Holidays in the Colourful Pyrénées
    Business – from Bath) —
It's a little village, Montségur and those happy Bathtimes are
    not forgot.

I was there in the Bookshop on my last morning in Montségur,
and what's good about that shop is that it doesn't arse
    around: —
In that Bookshop they only have books on the heresy —
Comics! (They take comics very seriously in France) —
You can bone up on the Cathar heresy (enough to do a show at
    the National Theatre I would have thought) by reading
    comics —
There are some marvellous ones: *Le Diable et les Cathares* —
And in *Le Chemin de Montségur*,[46] a panel:
laughing heretics in the fire, and the representative of the
    Church of Rome
(we Cathars call it the Synagogue of Satan) shouting:
'Brûlez Cathares! Brûlez!'[47] —
and the heretics going: 'Ah! Ah! Ah! Ah!' —
(French for 'Ha! Ha! Ha! Ha!') – 'Aceeedio!' —
Terrific!

The man in the Bookshop was very impressed that I was
    intending to learn all about the heresy from comics —
He told me that what I'd really need if I was going to get into
    it was Volumes 1, 2, 3 and 4 of *Les Chants de Pyrène*[48] —
These are the stories actually told round the fire by the Cathar
    minstrels —
It starts off with the story of the Pyrénées, and Pyrène —
Pyrène's a lady —

what happened evidently is that Hercules was wandering
   through this relatively flat area and bumped into this dame
   called Pyrène —
He gave her a good charvering (charmingly drawn) and then
   carried on his way —
then he thought, 'Here, actually I love her!' —
but when he went back she'd been eaten up by bears —
He was so pissed off he started heaving rocks around —
and that is the Pyrénées.

Anyway, I'd got this whole pile of books and comics I was
   going to buy,
and then I'd found *Burlesque et obscénité* with 'Song of
   Fotedor' —
and then this . . . (?)[49] . . . when —
into the shop came a beautiful French woman —
in shorts cut down from jeans, with severely pulled-back
   hair —
But what was *weird*, she came in and went straight to my pile
   of books and she pulled out Volume 2 of *Les Chants de
   Pyrène* —
I looked, and there were no more 2s – just 1s, 3s and 4ses —
I said to her: 'Je veux acheter ces livres. C'est mon columne
   de livres' —
I said to the homme, had he got any more deuxes and he said
   non —
and she wouldn't give it up —
He rang up another bookshop (which in any event was about
   fifty miles away)
and they hadn't got a 2 either —
I said, 'Well can I take a picture of you with my book?' —
'Certainement,' she said and she *posed* with my book, then
   suggested that we went outside for another snap where the
   light was better! —
(saucy trout!)[50] —
then she paid for my book and went off with it in her car.

I thought, I'm not going to let her get away with that! —
I know what I'll do, I'll put an ad in the International *Loot* —
in the French one – in the Desperately Seeking Suzanne
  section —
saying I'm wanting to contact the lady who on August 28th,
  1995,
bought Volume 2 of *Les Chants de Pyrène* at the little
  Bookshop, Montségur,
Bookshop Georges Servus, under the caff —
had her picture taken by a bald-headed gent, 'you're to get in
  touch' —
Why? Because, because – because the photograph has won an
  award! —
and I want to share the winnings with you – No, that's not
  right! —
Not right that she gets my book and sent some money too –
  NO! —
What I'll do is . . . I know what I'll do! When I get home I'll
  get hold of a load of those ladies' fashion shop-window
  dummy things, and dress them all up like her, put mock-ups
  of *Les Chants de Pyrène* in their hands, and then I'll stick
  them all around Stamford Hill where I live and I'll take arty
  sepia photographs of Hasidic Jews walking past them and
  not looking at them!
and listen! —
I'll get my photo of her blown up —
and stick it up as part of the set at the NT! [points at it] —
I'll get the press girl to get news of the whole bizarre biz into
  PARIS MATCH!!
And get 'em print these pics of her! —
Can't mess with me, like that . . .

And then, right then! is when Norman came (breathless) in —
'Which way she go?' —
'Dunno! Thataway! In a red car!' —
'FOT!' —

I've just thought – you're not going to get the full value out
 of this unless you know about the Old Man at the next table
 in the restaurant upstairs of the Bookshop – Who I knew
 from somewhere . . .

O Fot! Yes! OC Aye! We gotta do him, Norman . . .
He called me over . . .
When I was looking through the Guirdham books . . .
Did he say my name? —
I mean without me telling him . . . ? . . .

> '*I am not here for me to be –*
> *I'm here for you and me to be.*
> *I am here to create the space for you to be*
> *and I am here to be in the space that you create for me to*
>   *be.*'

I'll tell you where I heard those words:
1971 —
Victoria Palace, a couple of nights after Backster and his lie
 detectors —
a good-looking American giving an introductory lecture
to something or another —
He drew a circle, and he called it a pie —
and he cut a slice of pie, and he said:
'That slice is what we know that we know' —
and then he cut a bigger slice, and said:
'This slice here, is what we know that we don't know' —
'And all the rest,' he said, 'is what we don't know that we
 don't know' —
And evidently this was the area of his expertise —
I thought, 'Wow! It's a really weird[51] new form of humour
 this' —
He ran Human Growth Technology workshops in America —
I thought, 'I wouldn't mind going on one of those
and be able to talk like that!' —
But I didn't actually do anything about it.

But in 1975, I was approached by a radiant girl in a café —
She said, 'I'm ever so radiant, aren't I?' —
I said: 'Yes' —
Apparently I'd be radiating if I did what she'd just done —
The more she was talking, a thought came to my mind —
I cut a small slice out of her bun and I said:
'Say this is what we know that we know . . .' —
'Oh,' she said, 'have you done it?' —
'No,' I said, 'but I have heard that guy —
I saw him perform at the Victoria Palace – he was very
    funny' —
'Well, he's coming to London!' she said. 'You can go and be
    with him!' —
She told me how much it was —
It wouldn't sound that much now, but it'd be the equivalent of
    about £1000! —
'You're joking!' I said, 'I couldn't afford that!' —
She said: 'You gotta go! You sell your car! Sell your
    television! —
You gotta go *and you know so!'* —
Anyway, she said she'd give my number to Judy Valencic —
Judy Valencic rang me up and said: 'I hear you're interested in
    Erhard's Seminars Training?' —
I said, 'Well I saw him at the May lectures – he was very
    funny —
But I'm a bit daunted at the price' —
She said she'd arrange for an 'est' graduate to come round and
    check my things – work out what best to sell —
(I thought: this really is a new form of humour –)
And I thought, Well if it costs that anyway, it would be
    cheaper doing it here than going to the States —
So I said: 'Yeah – don't bother. I'll find the money
    somehow' —

They send you this: a brochure in Question and Answer form:

Q: What is the purpose of the est training?

A: The purpose of the est training is to transform your
ability to experience living so that the situations you have
been trying to change or have been putting up with, clear up
just in the process of life itself. Werner Erhard, founder of
est, said: 'Sometimes people get the notion that the purpose
of est is to make you better. It is not. I happen to think that
you are perfect the way you are . . . the problem is that
people get stuck acting the way they were, instead of being
the way they are.'
Q: Do you have to believe the training will work for the
training to work?
A: No. In fact many people go through most of the
training believing it won't work.
Q: In the training on offer, do you replace one kind of
belief with another kind of belief?
A: We replace believing with experiencing.

And it goes on:

Q: Why do my friends seem to have such difficulty
explaining how the training works?
A: Having someone tell you what it is like to parachute
out of an aeroplane is not the same as experiencing jumping
out of an aeroplane.
Q: What do I need to wear?
A: You should consider your own comfort, and the fact
that the training takes place in a hotel.

It was held in the ballroom of a hotel not far from Victoria
   Station —
two very long weekends —
and the first thing you have to do is fill in this form —
You've paid, but you now have to fill in a form —
One of the questions on the form is:
'What do you hope to achieve from the est training?'
So I wrote down: 'Insight into a new form of humour' —
I was about to go in when I was called over —

This bloke said, 'Oy! Did you write that?' —

I said, 'Yeah' —

'Well you can't go in with that' —

'Well that is why I'm here,' I said, 'I saw him performing at
   the Victoria Palace and he was very funny' —

He said, 'Are you married?' —

I said, 'No' —

He said, 'Do you live with anyone?' —

I said, 'No' —

He said, 'Are your mother and father alive?' —

I said, 'My Dad is and my Mum isn't' —

He said, 'When did your mother die?' —

I said, 'When I was twelve' —

He said, 'Did you complete that relationship?' —

?! —

He said, 'Did you complete your relationship with your
   mother?' —

I said, 'I don't know, I mean there would have been more to it
   if she hadn't of died' —

He said, 'Did you complete your relationship with your
   mother?' —

I said, 'No.'

He said, 'Well you could write that down' —

So I put down, 'I've come to complete my relationship with
   my mother' . . .

There were five hundred people all in this ballroom —

all in regular straight lines —

We weren't allowed to talk —

we had to sit there, facing the same way —

First on was Namib —

Namib had to get us to agree to the agreements —

We had to agree to a whole load of things before it would take
   place at all —

Things like: you mustn't have a watch on,

you mustn't take tape recordings, you mustn't take any
  notes —
We had to agree that if you wanted to 'share' you had to raise
  your hand, wait till you're acknowledged by the trainer,
  then wait for the microphone to be brought to you by an est
  graduate trustie —
Once you'd got the microphone you were to stand with it, and
  speak into the microphone holding it three inches from your
  mouth —
and Namib and trusties came round to check we all knew what
  three inches was,
(and it really was a shock for some people) —
Once you'd shared into the microphone you were to remain
  standing until the est graduate trustie came for the
  microphone —
And you weren't allowed to go to the toilet ('bathroom', he
  called it) except in designated 'bathroom breaks' —
Well, the thing is, people thought that was just *absurd* —
People were saying, 'Oh, come on!' —
(and it was getting rather terrific, because we'd really got this
  Namib on the run)
'You mean we can't go to the toilet unless it's a designated
  "go to the lavatory break" – is that actually what you're
  saying?!!' —
and he said: 'Yeah' —
'Why . . . ?' —
'Because Werner has found out that that is what works' —
(We were united now, getting at the awful Namib:)
'Well,' we said, 'it might work in America, but now you're in
  Great Britain! You can't just spring that on us! You don't
  know what we were doing yesterday. Some of us might
  have a weak this or a weak that! What do you expect us to
  do then mate? JUST SIT HERE AND POOH OUR
  PANTS?!!!'
Namib agreed that is what you would have to do —
Whaaat? —
and then suddenly, from behind us: —

'YAAAGH! YOU FUCKING ASSHOLES!!! —
AND ISN'T THAT WHY YOUR FUCKING RIDICULOUS
 LIVES DON'T WORK – AIN'T THAT WHY YOU'VE
 PAID A FORTUNE TO BE HERE! YOU MISERABLE
 ASSHOLES!!!!!' —
We now had two very handsome men on stage:
Werner Erhard and Ted Long, in their blazers —
Erhard so handsome I was scanning his face for a flaw —

You know that new lifeform that was found recently? —
the thing with three penises that only knows what to do with
 two of them, that was found on the hair of a lobster, on its
 lip?[52] —
Actually I found it back then in 1975 —
But you can only see it if he's passing close —
there on the Erhard lip —
Keep your gaze to that new life, is my advice! —

We started off with 'Is what's so, so?' —
Is so so? —
Is this chair this chair? —
We're not advanced here, we're not saying 'Is this chair *a*
 chair?' —
we're saying, 'Is this chair this chair?' —
Someone would say, 'Yes, to all intents and purposes' —
TO ALL INTENTS AND PURPOSES!!?? —
By *all* intents and purposes do you mean ALL intents and
 purposes? —
or are you implying a get-out? —
I'd guess (hadn't got a watch on) it takes about four hours to
 get five hundred people to agree that what is so is so —
Then Erhard in his blazer said:
'Yes. But not so obviously, it's also so what' —
Just along from me was an older gentleman of military bearing
 name-tagged JACK —
and Jack was beginning to rumble —

'I'd just like to say . . .' said Jack —

'Just a moment, Jack,' said Werner, 'I think we made an
 agreement didn't we? If you want to share, you raise your
 hand till acknowledged by the trainer' —

'Mn!' said Jack, and raised his hand —

But he wasn't acknowledged! He had his hand up for about
 half an hour! —

Eventually he's acknowledged —

'I would just like to say . . .' —

Wait for the microphone, Jack! Didn't we agree you had to
 stand, Jack?

Three inches, Jack! —

What he did actually say was amazing —

What he was was a Black Ops man —

He had tortured people and himself been tortured —

he knew what was going on here —

he knew about brain-washing techniques —

he knew about the dark and dirty end of fascism, did Jack —

and he let us all know —

And Ted and Werner heard him out, then Ted said:

'Thank you for sharing that with us, Jack' —

Then: 'The agreement is you remain standing, Jack, until the
 microphone is taken from you' —

Then they said: 'Now that's what you want to say . . .' —

'What?' —

'*What is it that you don't want to say Jack?*'

'Well, I could add this,' says Jack —

'No, hang on Jack. This is just going to be a few other things
 that you didn't happen to say. What is it you don't want to
 tell us, Jack?' —

Now, there's an order of gentleman you're not meant to find
 out about —

they are of granite —

we don't find out about them, do we? —

But they didn't let Jack go —

they had him there for two hours ($?^{53}$), and we found out all
  about Jack —
we found out about his daughter —
we found out about his *granddaughter* —
Then there came this moment: Erhard said:
'So, shall we dance with the listening, Jack, in a conversation
  for possibility!!' —
and Jack – it's like he didn't break down, he broke UP —
He sobbed —
a curious kind of whooping – 'Whooh! Whooh! Whooh!' —
The microphone was taken —
He sat down —
A neighbour reached out an arm to comfort him —
'LEAVE HIM ALONE!! GET HIM A BARF BAG!' —
Says Erhard: 'Would anyone else like to share?' —
And yes, this woman would! —
She did five minutes, then went into spasm:
'Uwuh, wuh, wuh, uwuh!!!' —
The form is, when anything happens like that, you applaud
  it —
'Thank you for sharing that with us, Jennifer' —
'Uwuh, wuh, wuh, uwuh!!!''
'Whooh! Whooh! Whooh!'

And loads more wanted a go! —
it was extraordinary, sometimes they just got up, took the
  microphone, and:
'Whaa! Whaa! Uwaahhh!!' —
I thought: I really wouldn't be anywhere else.

The next day, Jack hadn't run away —
he was there —
He was like some kind of hero now —
fine-looking women were coming up to him —
and **rubbing** him – ? —

Cutting through to the last Sunday now: —
And the whole business is this: 'Did you get it?' —
and we don't go until everyone's got it —
'Did you get it?' —
And if you get it it seems like a light bulb comes on in your
    head —
You radiate —
and all the ones who get it get to stand together
over the other side of the Ballroom —
'Got what?' I was thinking. 'I can't have been paying
    attention . . .' —
Suddenly it was my turn: 'Ken! Have you got it? Did you get
    it?' —
I said: 'Well, I don't know whether I've got it or not got
    it . . .' —
'You don't know whether you've got it or not got it? —
so that's what you got, so you got it' – ! —
I said: 'Is getting it just whatever you get?' —
He said: 'If that's what you got!' —
I thought, I can't face any more of this! —
So I joined the radiated —
and looking round at all these other radiating people . . . —
or *faking* radiance —
Had they really got it? Or had none of us got it?! —
The funny thing is, thinking <u>that</u> *actually made you radiate!*
Yeah. I got it.
est – an incredible mix of Zen, Dianetics, and Abbott and
    Costello —
Got it!
Terrific.

Following that, they're going to open the doors and about a
    thousand people who've done the training in America are
    going to rush in and *love* us —
But we don't know that yet —

First this last opportunity for anyone who didn't get to share to
    share now —
I raised my hand and the microphone was raced to me —
I said, 'I saw Werner performing at the Victoria Palace some
    years ago —
I thought he was very funny —
In a sense, I suppose I've been no less entertained here these
    two weekends —
I haven't shared because I don't feel my life is quite the same
    as everyone else's; it's been so wonderful hearing all this
    stuff coming up from people —
problems with their husbands, wives, kids and bosses —
But I work for myself and I live very contentedly alone, you
    see —
I say alone – that's not strictly true:
It's just me – and the ferrets' —
(I was breeding ferrets at the time for this hit act which
    consisted of putting live ferrets down your trousers for
    world-record lengths of time —
Sort of like putting your head in the lion's mouth, but a pocket
    edition) —
I said, 'If you have ferrets in the house like I do, you cannot
    designate the bathroom break of a ferret. They do tend to
    shit anywhere to start with, but in the end they narrow it
    down to about four or five places, and then you can put
    newspaper down there' —
But the Great Man didn't seem to know what a ferret was —
I explained they were long furry ferocious things for chasing
    up rabbits —
I said, 'I would like to share this: Last night when I went
    home . . .' —

I was referring now to an exercise we'd done a lot —
It's an exercise to help you in communication —
and it gives Ted and Werner a rest —

You have to look with both your eyes into the eye of a
partner —
for ages —
Hours, it seems (you wouldn't know, you don't get your watch
back till after) —
and they're doing the same to you —
And all you're doing is you're saying in your head:
'It's quite OK for me to be here, and it's quite OK for you to
be there' —
That's all you do – and you mustn't get anything else in your
head —
'It's quite OK for me to be here, and it's quite OK for you to
be there' —
Then comes the command: 'Change eyes!' —
Another half an hour in the other eye —
'It's quite OK for me to be here, and it's quite OK for you to
be there' —

Anyway, I said, 'When they shit, ferrets, you see,' I said,
'what they do is they sort of back up their long bodies —
It's a bit like backing up a lorry and trailer —
And when they do that, their backs arch and their heads go
up —
When it did it last night, one of them – just out of habit now,
I looked with both my eyes into the one eye of the ferret,
and I said to him ''It's quite OK for me to be here, and it's
quite OK for you to be there'' —
It had finished, done its business, but it stayed really for quite
a time doing the exercise' —
'Well thank you for sharing that with us Ken,' he said —
They hadn't come for the microphone —
! —
'Anything else?' he said —
'Yeah,' I said —
I thought: *OK you bugger* —

'The thing about ferrets is they like to go behind things, and last night one of the ferrets got behind the bookshelf and happened to knock out *Roget's Thesaurus* – it landed open at the page of "laughter" —

I was having a look at it, and did you know there's a snicker, a snigger, a smigger and a snork? And I thought, you really would be someone if you knew the difference' —

I tried them out: Huhuh, heheh, hihih . . .

'Just doing that, it was in a sense as if I not only left the room, I left the world!'

Huhuh, heheh, hihih, hahahah! —

(In fact the Laughing Fat Man with the Teeth had appeared during the proceedings and had been quite remarkable with his finger . . . but I chose not to get into that) —

'Anyway,' I said, 'when I got back, I thought: This est is terrific —

I don't want to join it and arse about running round with microphones or anything. But I'd like to have my own rival outfit —

Then I noticed that the ferret had knocked out another book: Frazer's *The Golden Bough* (abridged)[54] —

It was open at page 100:

In the thirteenth century arose the Brothers and Sisters of the Free Spirit, who held that any of us can become one with God and enjoy a glorious immunity from all laws. They presented a shocking air of lunacy. Those of highest spiritual life dispensed with clothes. Decency is characteristic of a soul that has not yet been elevated. Their progress was accelerated by the Inquisition, and they expired in the flames with triumphant cheerfulness.'[55]

I said: 'I think I'd go in kind of the opposite direction to est: —

The "Brothers and Sisters of the Free Spirit" . . . —

I'll call mine JEST' —

And actually, I'd been working on the brochure for it all night —

(and on it, the 'J' of JEST is made up out of a tumbling
ferret) —

Q: What is the purpose of the JEST training?
A: The purpose of the JEST training is to transform your
ability to sense the ludicrous in everything, so that every
situation you are in is seen as the jape of the century. Ken
Campbell, founder of JEST said: 'Sometimes people get
the notion that the purpose of JEST is to make you a
comedian. It is not. I happen to think you are hysterically
funny as you are. The problem is people get stuck seeing
how tragic they were, instead of how comic they are.'
Q: How much does it cost?
A: No money – in fact not even the price of the postage
for registering for it if you address the enclosed envelope to
Father Christmas, and write in a very childish hand.
Q: Will I be made to look ridiculous?
A: No. You will discover how ridiculous you already
look.
Q: Will I need Wellingtons?
A: Yes.
Q: Will we have to wear name tags?
A: Yes, but not your own.
Q: Will I be permitted to smoke?
A: Only during short specified periods of the Booger
Event when smoking is compulsory.

Werner said: 'Well thank you for sharing that with us Ken,
and good luck with your JEST' —
But still nobody came for the microphone —
(a bit of a worry because I'd run out of material now) —
He said: 'Did you write the letter?' —
I said: 'Yes' —
This refers to a bit of homework we had to do —
You had to write to a departed one —
Not to send off, but just as a personal growth exercise,
to complete your relationship —
'Who did you write it to?' —

'. . . I wrote it to a dog I once had as a kid that ran away, a
mongrel called Tim with brown cheeks that ran away and
got run over. I told Tim that I now took full responsibility
for him running away' —
He said: 'Anything else?' —
I said, 'And a couple of notes to some mice' —
He said, 'Can I see the letter?' —

Now the thing was, I hadn't done that at all actually —
I'd written a letter to my Mum —
I said: 'No, because in the last all-too-brief bathroom break,
the only cubicle available had run out of paper' —
Werner now looking at me with both his eyes staring into my
weaker eye —
(I had my two eyes fixed on that three-penised bit of new
life) . . .
'Thank you for sharing that with us Ken' —
Hey! I got away with it!! —
Then all the thousand people rush in and love us —
And people were coming up to me and asking:
'Is this for real? Are you really going to run a JEST Humour
Workshop?' —
I said: 'Yeah. I am' —
'Terrific Ken!' (Werner!) 'Legendary sharing!
Permission to write about you in the est magazine?
Only read by staff and graduates . . . ?' —
'Yes.'
I was moved.
Jack came up, he said he wanted to come on my JEST —

I had about twenty people showed up —
I got proper replies back to Father Christmas, in childish
hands —
Anyway, they came and they filled in their forms and were
sent back because they weren't ludicrous enough —
and then we were all in —

Sadly Jack didn't come —
But I'll tell you who did —
I'm not a sizeist, but this dame was beyond what the word
  'tubby' would convey —
Her tree-trunk legs . . .
'Under the spreading chestnut tree'! —
A short-sighted Damanhurian would have plugged her up and
  expected music . . .
And she was really grim —
You see I hadn't thought it through that someone would turn
  up who was really in need of the training —
Apparently she was an under-headmistress —
I was trying to get them going with the difference between a
  snicker, a snigger, a smigger and a snork —
and under-headmistress was sinking it under —
And I thought, 'Right! I'll bring forward the Booger
  Event!' —

(I had this notion that actually possibly everything is funny —
But you're blocked, you see —
'I find Frankie Howerd funny, I don't find Benny Hill
  funny . . .' —
Well it seemed to me that in a humour workshop
you want to find as much funny as possible —
It's like there's a wall between you and the everything
  funny —
and so as a group we were going to dismantle the wall,
and then GO THROUGH —
and arse around in the 'everything funny' for a bit –) —

But Broad of Beam was blocking the whole show.
The Booger Event is in a book, Seekers, called *Technicians of
  the Sacred*[56] —
and it's weird rituals and things that primitive tribes lay on —
people who haven't had the wit to invent theatre yet —

but nonetheless do gather together and carry on in
   extraordinary ways —
like 'The Going Round Grease Event' of the Asiatic
   Eskimos —
Anyway, I read out a few of the tamer ones, then said:
'Now we'll try one, shall we? —
We'll do the Cherokee Indian Booger Event' —
It goes like this:

Booger Event
*Participants: A number of four to ten or more masked men
(called 'boogers'), occasionally a couple of women
companions. Each dancer is given a personal name, usually
obscene; for example: Black Man, Black Ass, Frenchie, Big
Balls, Asshole, Rusty Asshole, Burster (penis), Swollen
Pussy, Long Prick, Sweet Prick, Piercer, Fat Ass, Long-
Haired Pussy, Etcetera.*
*Prelude: The dancers enter. The audience and the dancers
break wind.*
*First action: The masked men are systematically malignant.
They act mad, fall on the floor, hit at the spectators, and
push the men spectators as though to get at their wives and
daughters, etc.*

Jumping on to the Third Action, which was to be the sensation
of the morning:

*Booger Dance Song. The name given to the booger should
be taken as the first word of a song. This is repeated any
number of times, while the owner of the name dances a solo,
performing as awkward and grotesque steps as he possibly
can. The Audience applauds each mention of the name,
while the other dancers indulge in exhibitionism, e.g.
thrusting their buttocks out and occasionally displaying
toward the women in the audience large phalli concealed
under their clothing. These phalli may contain water which
is then released as a spray.*

(These I provided –) —

I said, 'We'll let the names for the boogers . . .' —

(everyone was going to be a booger) 'We'll let the names
   come organically' —

So that we'd chant, say, 'Big Balls, Big Balls, Big Balls,'

and look round the circle wondering who it is . . .

He knows who he is! —

'Big Balls, Big Balls, Big Balls' —

and the person who knew he was Big Balls would eventually
   come out —

and do the dance of Big Balls.

And then we got to Fat Arse.

There wasn't a lot of looking round needed —

'Fat Arse, Fat Arse, Fat Arse' – and it was a very demanding
   rhythm —

'Fat Arse, Fat Arse, Fat Arse' —

And Tree had to step in the middle and acknowledge it was
   her! —

But she seemed to think that merely acknowledging it was
   enough —

In no way was it! —

'Fat Arse, Fat Arse, Fat Arse, Fat Arse, Fat Arse, Fat
   Arse!!' —

We wouldn't let Lady Beerbohm go —

We kept going —

'Fat Arse, Fat Arse, Fat Arse, Fat Arse, Fat Arse, Fat
   Arse!!' —

Then it was as if something came into her and she
   DANCED —

She was wild —

'Fat Arse, Fat Arse, Fat Arse, Fat Arse, Fat Arse, Fat
   Arse!!' —

Slinging her fat around —

It looked likely she would have a coronary within the next
   minute! —

'Fat Arse, Fat Arse, Fat Arse, Fat Arse, Fat Arse, Fat
   Arse!!' —

But we had to see it to the end —
Because? Because . . . Because! —
WHAT WAS THE COURT CASE GOING TO BE
   LIKE. . . ?! —
But she beat us! —
We couldn't shout 'Fat Arse' any more —
We went off for an early lunch break in the pub —
She was the darling of the day! Everyone fell in love with Fat
   Arse —
and **rubbed** her —
And she fell in love with us —
and rubbed us back —
But I'll tell you what's interesting —
'Booger' is not a Cherokee Indian word . . .

You know how in Australia now you're not really anybody
   unless you can trace yourself back to a convict? —
It's kind of the same in Newfoundland —
except there you have to trace yourself back to a pirate —
or even better: you trace yourself back to a heretic —
In the thirteenth century when the Catholics were burning all
   the heretics in Montségur, Toulouse, Carcassonne —
Cathars (also known as Albigensians and Acadians), and
   across the Balkans where they were known as Bogomils
   (they were the Holy Buggers – the Boogars, the Bogie
   Men), escaped first into Bulgaria (which in its day was
   known as 'Buggerarea') and then, guided by the mysterious
   Portolano maps, escaped across the Atlantic (way before
   Columbus), settling first in Newfoundland, then Halifax,
   Nova Scotia, some saying that they took with them the Holy
   Grail (smuggled out the back of Montségur during the
   siege) —

Some fine books on that subject: e.g. *Holy Grail Across the
   Atlantic*[57] —
(I can tell you where the Holy Grail[58] is:

it's sixty miles out of Halifax, Nova Scotia, and it's down a
   thing known as the Money Pit on Oak Island, Mahone
   Bay) —

When the British and French arrived properly to plant their
   flags and found all these dreadful OC-speaking heretics
   there, they slung 'em out —
(Longfellow wrote a moving poem on the whole thing called
   'Evangeline' —
You know that vast amounts of Canada are called Acadie? —
That came from the cry of heretics as they laughed from the
   flames —
'Acedio!' – it kinda meant 'See, I got it right!' —
The Catholics thought up a whole new sin called Acedianism:
the sin of laughing at your punishment —
In St Johns I picked up this book: *Last of the Moe Haircuts*:
   *The Influence of the Three Stooges on Twentieth-Century
   Culture*[59] —
And here, look, in Chapter 12: The Influence of the Three
   Stooges on the Modern Papacy —
A quote:

> Certainly Larry's willingness to haul himself around by his
> own earlobe, to yank out great hunks of his own hair, to
> knock himself on the forehead with his own fist, was in
> direct line with the ancient tradition of self-flagellation and
> mortification of the flesh. Larry's use of the expression 'Ah
> kid'ya not' may or may not have been his own voicing
> of the medieval prohibition against acedia . . .

When the Acedians (Bogomils/Cathars) were booted out of
Halifax,
some went and founded the city of Montreal —
others to Louisiana and were known as the Cajuns
   (Acedians) —
they of course bumped into Cherokee Indians —

and taught them the Booger Event —
The magnificent Booger Event was originally Cathar.

Home —
A lot of people would claim that they live in their home —
and that must be terrific —
I quite like it where I live (Stamford Hill, North London) —
but it's not my home —
So what do I mean by 'home'? —
It's the place your mind goes when you're not doing
    anything —
My home is St Johns, Newfoundland —
Newfoundland is a large island, the first part of America
    discovered —
(The Vikings rowed there) —
So if I close my eyes, that's where I see —
In my head my home is 56 Freshwater Road —
Ed Riche's spare room —
St Johns —
'Noofndlaand' —
I took to going there eight or nine years ago, doing my shows
    for them —
I perform 'em in the Longshoremen's Protective Union
    Hall —
They're my best, brightest audience there —
I'll tell you why —
My last show, *Mystery Bruises*, which demonstrates how
    quantum mechanics proves you must only do comedy
    now —
they were the only audience that got *everything* —
They're so cut off they hadn't heard that you only have to *buy*
    Stephen Hawking's book —
they'd all **read** it! —
and debated it through the long arctic winter —

These days, Newfoundland is basically a bunch of Irishmen
  who found somewhere worse to live —
I know more people in St Johns than I know in all the rest of
  the world put together —
They've got this mnemonic trick so you don't forget them:
'Hi!' says this lady you've never met before in the Ship Inn
  off Duckworth, 'I'm Trudy the vicar's daughter and I've
  still got half a bag of Magic Mushrooms, picked by my
  brother Tom last year on Signal Hill' —
'Hi! I'm Pete, and I've just been putting everything I own into
  boxes' —
'Hi! I'm Frank, one of the Barry Cousins —
We come from the poor side of town which is how come we
  dance so well!' —
'Hi! I'm Melody Lane, a songwriter/singer —
My next album is all songs about the sphincter —
Say you hold a mix of gas, liquid and solid in your hands
and then just try and let out the gas —
No matter how clever you are, you can't do it —
But the sphincter ani can! —
The sphincter can tell the difference between gas, liquid and
  solid —
The sphincter knows whether you're on your own or with
  someone —
It knows if you've got your pants up or down —
It's the sphincter holds together the Dignity of Man' —
I said I knew a splendid lady who danced under the name of
  Fat Arse —
'Can you put us in touch?' —
(In just a few minutes you feel you've come home.)

In some of the bars, you can have either ice cubes or 'Bergie-
  Bits' —
Bergie-Bits are pieces of genuine iceberg —
the novelty is, they sink in your drink —

Back home in St Johns we don't use our taxis for going places
   much —
Basically they're off-licences —
You simply ring up the cab firm and give them your order:
'Case of Buds, bottle of whiskey, bottle of Screech' —
Screech is the local rum —
To become an Honorary Newfoundlander you drink a bottle of
   Screech then, to the accompaniment of wild fiddle music,
   you fuck a cod —
(I must put up my certificate) —

Place-name derivation is not a study permitted in Newfound-
   land till the Sixth Form, most names being pirate in
   origin, and often quite obscene —
Like the little out-port town of Shove-Her-Tickles —
Up-Yer-Fancy —
I've got a snap of myself under the sign of the little town of
   Dildo —
A few years ago a 'Yup' couple moved into Dildo —
made themselves really busy —
Wasn't it about time everyone here grew up? —
Maybe we should change the name and thus increase property
   values? —
So they forced a referendum on changing the name —
Only the Yup couple voted for change —
The Mayor of Dildo said, as he announced the result:
"'Twas our piratical forebears in their wisdom who called it
   here Dildo,
in the hope we'd keep the real pricks out' —
(The Yup couple got the message and went) —

I thought I might settle in Dildo —
I ask: 'What's our industry in Dildo?' —
'We're wreckers, Ken!' —

'What, you mean we wait for a ship to wreck and then go and
  salvage it?'
'Yeah . . . except we don't necessarily *wait*.'

Newfoundland was a British colony (our first, I think) —
then they were independent —
Then in 1947 came the notion of confederating with
  Canada —
the Newfs asked Westminster for advice —
But behind the scenes behind the scenes behind the scenes —
(this is the way they talk about it in St Johns) —
Ottawa went to Westminster and said:
'Deliver Newfoundland unto us, and we'll wipe out a vast
  chunk of the War Debt' —
So Britain moved in to run the vote as to whether to
  confederate or not —
It was close, but the vote eventually came out as 51 per cent to
  49 in favour of confederating —
But if you get an expert, like Mike Jones, Ed Riche[60] (in fact
  anyone there I've ever met), they'll point out this:
The whole of Newfoundland is about the size of West
  Germany —
but there's only half a million people live there —
we kinda know who everyone is . . .
When they saw those votes coming in from the little out-ports,
there's no chance at all they voted for confederation, those last
  votes.

The Cheat Confederation went ahead —
Refrigerators arrived! (awfully handy for the two weeks of
  summer) —
televisions came! (with the promise of programmes sometime
  if the Newfs were good) —
But the only sense for being on Newfoundland (economically)
  is the fish —

What Ottawa was up to was seeking to discourage the Newfs
from fishing their fish —

To fish their mighty stocks of cod, Newfs now needed a
licence – progressively more difficult to obtain and
penalties increasingly stringent —

Ottawa was trying to get the Newfs to give up the ports and
settle the bleak interior.

They came up with some creative schemes to persuade the
Newfs to move inland —

e.g. the five-mile-wide Mink Ranch —

Then the question:

What to feed umpteen million mink? —

Answer: whales —

They started with the big 'uns and fished out all the blue
whales from the area —

and started fishing them down in size until they got to number
five:

the Minke whale —

Everyone thought, Why didn't we think of it before? —

Obviously the Good Lord called them 'Minke whales' because
they're meant to be fed to mink! —

But a curious thing happens when you feed Minke whale to
mink:

Minke meat makes mink go manky —

the fur falls out in tufts and hanks —

Even worse to tell you:

Minke-fed manky mink shit completely contaminates the
area —

a moose passing over the area'd get completely alopeciaed by
the time it got to the other side —

the whole site had to be fenced off like that Scottish anthrax
island.

What Ottawa was up to was selling the fishing rights to the
Japanese, Portuguese, and a load of other eses —

who came along with their three-mile-wide trawling nets —

sometimes these break free (they don't degrade) —
they carry on marauding the depths —
It's called 'dead fishing' —
You get to the point we achieved three years ago:
ALL THE COD HAS GONE —
and the experts say they won't be coming back —
Newf authors write books with clear and simple titles these
    days:
Surviving Confederation —
and *No Fish – And Our Lives*[61] . . .

It's made overall economic sense to put ninety per cent of a
    population on Welfare.
Ed Riche says: 'There's only Zen reasons for being here
    now' . . .

I'll tell you, actually there's a lot of reasons to be there —
if you've ever sat round a Newfoundland fireside in your
    warm little house in the Arctic winter with five foot of snow
    outside . . .
Everyone seems to play the violin or the guitar out there, or
    the banjo or the squeezebox —
everyone back home's a comedian —
not professionally, exactly —
it's more a case of whose turn it is now —
whose 'Time'.

Last time I was home there was a thing called SNAG: —
Say No to American Garbage —
the Americans had come up with this terrific idea —
really nothing at all happening with the interior of
    Newfoundland —
Why not bomb it and hollow the whole thing out and make it a
    mighty dustbin for America's rubbish?[62] —
There was a bit of attraction here for the Newfs:

they say, 'Well, we'll be bin-men! Let's be positive about
  it! —
We'll be merry singing heigh-ho bin-men! It could be
  OK!' —
Then they learnt that quite a lot of the garbage was gonna be
  kinda *specialised* —
beyond the wit of the locals to bin —
And so there was a petition to sign —
The lady taking the signatures said: 'This is going to be more
  difficult to save than cuddly stuff like bats and whales. This
  is a place where nothing grows, where nobody goes. We're
  fighting here for the rights of a complete Fuck-Allness to be
  left in peace.'
I found it stirring —
I signed, and gave generously.

On the last night I was there, after I'd done my quantum
  mechanical humour show, I was with a couple of friends:
  the brother and sister of Andy Jones[63]:
Mike and Cathy Jones —
Mike Jones makes movies now —
in fact he made a terrific movie called *Secret Nation* which
  was all about the cheating of the confederation vote —
and I was in it and played the Brit who knew —
Mike was a monk till he was thirty when he started to get
  curious about mature women —
It was a paedophilic order with a male bias, so he was asked to
  leave —
Anyway, Mike was there, and his sister Cathy —
Cathy Jones is the reigning Queen of Canadian Comedy —
she's got two TV shows and broadcasts across the Canadian
  nation —
she's a bit like Tracey Ullman was when we had her —
Actually, what she's really like is the young Martha Raye —
Cathy was out the back cooking (she's a great cook) —

Mike was saying to me, 'Have you heard about
   ''affirmations'', Ken?' —
'Yeah,' I said, 'I have, I think, if you're talking about that sort
   of New Age businesses. I've heard you can affirm for
   anything —
If you're constipated, then every day you write down:
''Glorious poos flow triumphantly'' – write it down a
   thousand times, and within the month, you're Mr Regular –
   get yourself on the cover of Health Magazines' —
Mike said: 'I hadn't heard about it like that —
I'm talking about affirming a person into your life' . . .

Apparently it had been late one night and he'd been sitting up
   drinking with Cathy, and he'd got his notebooks out, his
   diaries, and he'd said:
'D'you know Cathy, I haven't been laid for a year' —
Cathy said: 'Why don't you try affirming a woman in then
   Mike?' —
And he hadn't known what she meant —
(Apparently that's what Cathy does —
she likes to live with a bloke, but not for more than a year —
she finds they run out of steam —
so then she simply affirms a new one in –) —
It's evidently an ancient practice there, probably dating back
   to the heretics —
another term they have for it now is 'Coincidence
   Manipulation' —
What you do is this:
You write down on a piece of paper:
'Coming into my life now is . . .' —
and then you describe (in the present tense) everything about
   this person —
what they look like —
how tall they are, the sort of clothes they wear and so on —
what books they've read, what movies they've seen —
everything —

'If you find yourself describing someone you already know,'
  says Mike —
'Well then you know what to do, don't you? You ring her up
  and say:
"Hi Phyllis, I'm just affirming you up here, so you better get
  on over" ' —
The trick, says Mike, is to leave nothing to chance,
be as specific and detailed as possible —
you can't cross anything out (that's one of the rules) —
once it's written, 'tis writ —
and then when you're finished and it's no one you know for
  sure —
you write: 'And I welcome this person into my life' —
and you sign it, and date it —
'And then what do you do?' —
'Well, you're done then,' says Mike. 'You just stick it
  somewhere —
You stick it on top of your wardrobe' —
And then, according to Cathy, the affirmed person will come
  into your life within fourteen days —
'So did you do it?' I said —
'Yeah,' says Mike —
'And what happened?' —
'On the eighth day she came' —
'What do you mean "she came"?' —
'Well, she was just kinda passing' —
The picture I got was that some woman, approximating his
  description, had been passing his window and Mike had
  nipped out and introduced himself —
and he got a date and he took her out that night —
the next night he took her to dinner and she was checking
  out! —
she was spot on: she'd read that book! (not many people
  have) —
on the third night he brought her home —
he said: 'Sit down here Hilda' —

he went upstairs and got his affirmation down off the
    wardrobe, read the whole thing to her —
And she said: 'Well I go along with all of that Mike' —
I said: 'So you live with Hilda now then, Mike?' —
'Well, no I don't, Ken,' he said, 'because I neglected to write
    down:
''She will have a positive attitude to my drinking and
    smoking'' —
That's why,' he says, 'Cathy's sometimes funny about you —
A while ago, when she was affirming a new one in, she
    affirmed for a bald-headed witty geezer, but you never
    showed up' —
'She knows me!' I said, 'Why didn't she give me a ring?' —
'I dunno,' he said, 'maybe she thought he had to come from
    Montreal or something . . . But that's why she sometimes
    looks at you a bit funny' —
By this time she'd affirmed this Buddhist into her life —
Not an oriental. One of the Drinking Buddhists of Halifax,
    except her one doesn't drink much, which was exactly what
    she'd affirmed for, thinking, herself, at the time, of signing
    the pledge —
But tonight he was off bonging . . .

Cathy brings in the meal and we tuck in —
then the whiskey and the Screech —
Cathy said to me: 'Aren't you lonely, Ken?' —
and I thought, Well yeah, I wouldn't mind doing my year with
    Cathy —
'Lonely?' I said. 'No, I don't think I'm lonely —
I'm alone, certainly, but I don't think I'm lonely —
I mean it has been experimented with, you know, living with
    me —
but it's maybe not that easy —
See, you gotta remember I was an only child, Cathy —
my Mum died when I was twelve —
I'm extremely used to my own company —

the problem is, I can imagine people much better than they
actually turn out to be —
more courageous, more curious, more comical, more
convenient —
To hang around with me, Cathy, you would have to be better
than *nothing* —
See, Cathy, the problem is I never grew up —
grew old, to be sure, but not up . . .
I don't know what growing up is, actually —
It seems to me that when people get to a certain age they feel
they've got to assemble for themselves a character from a
rather restricted shelf of officially recognised bits and
pieces . . .
See, I have no fabricated ego, loud with answers —
nor no Buddhist egolessness bonged out by gongs . . .
I feel the same now as I did forty years ago:
just running round like a dog in the wrong house —
I haven't got the talent the others have got for belonging
together —
They know:
where to go —
what to do —
who to vote for —
how VAT works —
what the Footsie Index is —
I can't even be bothered to guess —
All I bother with, Cathy, is those who *radiate* but don't seem
to know it . . .
Who are they out there Cathy? —
I mean, somewhere in that bit between Toddlerhood and
Adulthood, they must have had their moment of *sanity* . . .
When they saw the nodding man with the teeth . . .
and finger . . .
or whatever —
But 999,999 out of a million haven't got the grasp or grip to
hang on to that sanity —

to honour it —
to remember it even . . .' —

Mike Jones said:
'Mankind will not evolve until we take every coincidence as
    meant' —
I said: 'Meant by what?' —
He said: 'We won't know till we do it' —
Mike's interruption intrigued, but by then I was in some sort
    of flow —
'Cathy,' I said, 'I don't know what happens then, maybe it's
    the pressure of the herd forces 'em to suppose that the being
    that they were born to be is too odd for use[64] – So they
    quickly go to that restricted shelf of officially sanctioned
    bits and pieces to assemble themselves a character so that
    they can "function normally", and avoid arrest . . .' —
(whiskey and wisdom flowing freely now) —
'Who are they out there, Cathy? —
They're the SAS – the Storm Troopers of Cliché! —
They don't think —
they just echo —
they put all their energy into throwing away who they are in
    the interests of being everybody else' —
Cathy said: 'I think you need a partner, Ken.'

So they brought me pen and paper to see the kind of partner I
    should have —
This is what I wrote:
'Coming into my life now is a comedy partner' —
I thought that was cunning! —
'She has a pretty but funny face. Basically beautiful but she
    can twist it grotesquely' —
This well describes Cathy —
'She is funny and fun.
She thinks I'm funny.
She thinks my shows are funny.

But OUR shows are funnier.

She is into weirdness.

Unlike me she is sensitive to what people are thinking and
feeling' —

(That's actually just some bollocks that Cathy claims) —

All I was doing really was describing the hostess in general
terms —

I wasn't going to say: 'and she has a thirteen-year-old
daughter called Mara'!

I wrote: 'She has a background of water' —

(getting closer) —

'A background of *pirates*' —

And then:

'She is the toast of St Johns' – oops!

That didn't go down well —

I think there's a thing you could call 'Offensive
Familiarity' —

See, I thought of these people as my real family – my real
home —

And mainly it does seem like that —

But —

'The Toast of St Johns'. . . ? —

Maybe for some reason it wasn't given to me to say that —

I remember years ago I was in a pub with young Bob
Hoskins —

(Incidentally, good of Bob, wasn't it, to come all the way back
from Hollywood to tell us what to do with our phones) —

Anyway, we'd got talking to this American Vietnam
Veteran —

He was telling us tales of his time 'in 'Nam' —

And Bob said: 'So how long were you in 'Nam?' —

And I thought: 'You can't say *'Nam*, Bob! —

That's Offensive Familiarity!' —

The mood was darker —

Cathy said: 'What will you do about her sullen moods, Kenneth?' —

I said: 'I shall be creative with them Cathy. I can eventually find a way to turn them creatively' —

'Write it down then,' said Mike —

'Do you love her?' says Cathy —

See, they're different from us —

they can talk about love in a head-on way —

I went all British —

I said: 'Love her? . . . er . . . yes . . . well . . . yes . . . YES . . . but . . . But I don't *need* her' —

'Does she love you?' —

'. . . yes . . . But she doesn't *need* me' —

'What keeps you bowling along together then, Kenneth?' —

'Maybe not being able to answer that question, Cathy' —

'So the mystery of what binds you together binds you together . . . ?' —

'Mmm' —

'How long does it last?' —

'Maybe it's one of those things that goes on forever:

it always was —

it is now —

and it always will be —

but on the other hand, maybe it's just the space between heartbeats'[65] —

Cathy said: 'Coincidence cannot be manipulated by poetry, Kenneth' —

'That's not poetry,' said Mike. 'It's a fine answer' —

Cathy: 'OK. Describe her in detail . . . For example you haven't said whether or not she's in a wheelchair . . . ?' —

'!?' —

'I'm just pointing out how unspecific you've been —

So far your Affirmation is, shall we say, DRAUGHTY —

Does she cook well?' —

'Yes' —

She said: 'Does her practising the violin in the middle of the
    night drive you up the wall?' —
'In no way!' I said. 'In no way does it! I love her violin-
    playing —
In fact, the violin-playing becomes the cornerstone of our
    comedy routines together —
I haven't heard *you* practising the violin lately, Cathy . . .'
'That's because I don't play the violin, Kenneth —
So shall we quit horsing around now, and suppose you
    describe for us this violin-playing lady of your
    dreams! —
Colour of hair?' asks Cathy —
'Black' — (Cathy's is brown)
'Height?' —
'Five foot' — (Cathy is five foot six)
'Where's she from?' —
'Burma, Thailand, China – some place like that . . . a BORN
    Buddhist!' —
(Hey! Where's all this coming from?!) —
'How old?' —
'Not old' —
'How old's not old?' —
'Thirty isn't old, for example,' I said —
'Sure isn't. Have you got a pet name for her?' —
'Pud' —
'Has she got a pet name for you?' —
'Yes,' I said. 'Uncle' —
'What animal comes to mind?' —
'Ferret!'

Mike Jones was keeping the score here —
'So basically,' he said, 'it's a funny-looking, pretty, five foot,
    not old, oriental, violin-playing, a born Buddhist humorist,
    into weirdness, who, tho' sensitive, doesn't object to you
    calling her Pud . . .' —
'Not eventually,' I said —

'. . . background of pirates, essence of ferret, and the Toast of
St Johns' —

I signed and dated it and wrote: '. . . and I welcome this
person into my life' —

I had never encountered any Orientals in Newfoundland —
There is a Chinese restaurant in St Johns, but I think that's just
some locals who read a book —
(I have heard tales of Captain Ho who hunts the seals —
not for coats, you'll be pleased to hear —
But for their penises —
for 'Chinese Seal Penis Tea'.)

Next day, time to leave the folks back home and return to
where I live, beneath Stamford Hill —

And there was a message on the answerphone —
A film company wanting to know if I'd be in an educational
film for primary school kids to be shown on the box in
school hours —
about the inadvisability of very small children arsing around
with severely loony old men —
Was I interested in playing the lead? —
A script was biked round, and it was OK, and so I said yeah —

But then, preparing to set off for the first morning's filming,
the director had agreed that I could disguise for the part —
otherwise you get kids heaving bricks at you and thinking
they're gonna get a medal for it —
So I took some elements of disguise along with me —
It was all being filmed on a farm —
and to be called 'The Egg Man' because this old man I was
playing kept chickens and sold eggs —

(a front for his foul practices —
it's all explained in the teacher's pack) —
I took along my Mellors, for example —
these are David Mellor Disgraced Heritage Minister Teeth —
I had them done when he was first disgraced (toe-sucking) —
They're good, the Mellors —
they give you the look of perhaps going to be witty in a
    minute —
The wardrobe lady got quite inspired by 'em —
She said: 'Maybe the Egg-Man doesn't wear a hat, maybe he
    wears a tea-cosy!' —
The director was off in the fields filming with the little kids
    that I later have to molest —
so I set off to find him to get approval for the tea-cosy and
    Mellors look —
As I came down the steps of the make-up caravan —
there —
in the field —
was this five-foot oriental lady —
and she looked at me —
and she said: 'You look terrific!' —
I've never had anyone be that enthusiastic about the way I
    looked – *ever!*
I went and showed myself to the director and he said I looked
    fine —
he said I should have a prosthetic 'wen', i.e. a lump on my
    head that came through the cosy's spout-hole 'to JUSTIFY
    the cosy' —
and the oriental lady was still hanging around —
Being so short, she was 'stand in' for the little kids —
(if the kids aren't actually acting, they have to be in a caravan
    doing school work) —

Her name is Thieu-Hoa, pronounced like the question to
    which the answer might be 'Coffee!': 'Tea or Wha'?' —
I took her to excellent free location lunch —

She was from Haiphong in North Vietnam (Buddhist ✓) —
a boat refugee —
When the Americans left, they put about the notion that the
Chinese were helping the Vietnamese —
The Chinese were actually waiting to invade —
They just didn't want the place with awful Americans in it —
and as soon as the Yanks had gone, they started moving in —
and her Dad was Chinese —
One night, the family had abandoned house and off in open
boat on the South China Seas —
She was six then (she's now twenty-three) (very not old) —
she fell in at one point and was able to *breathe* under water —
She's had a previous life —
she was a plant that didn't bloom —
but not on this planet —
Would she bloom now? —
Well, she'd have to get on with it because fortune tellers had
told her she was going to die when she was thirty-five –
'More than two[66] fortune tellers!' —
Anyway, while they were afloat, they were all kidnapped by
PIRATES! —
And more! —
*really by profession she was an ORCHESTRAL
VIOLINIST!!* —
This was the eighth day of my Affirmation! —

She was very pretty, but while she was talking her eyes kinda
crossed —
and she showed me the impression of a pig she could do —
She could sing tragical traditional Vietnamese plaints (ethnic
cat-strangling) which certainly had comedy potential —
(P'raps preceeded by a Rambling Sid Rumpo-style intro?) —
I asked her if she'd like to try doing a comedy show with
me —
she said: 'Yeah – why not?' —

she was up for it as long as it didn't interfere with her
   orchestral or quartet engagements —
I think, Wow! Is it all as easy as this!? You just write down
   what you want, stick it on top of your wardrobe, and you get
   it!? —
'Toast of St Johns . . .' —
I ask her if she's ever been to Newfoundland —
'In Australia is it?' she asks —
So that bit obviously refers to the future . . .
I said to come to Amsterdam —
doing the Quantum Mechanical Humour Show in a little venue
   there . . .
She came —
And she laughed lots; and wonderfully —
she cackles like several old men down a drain —
I'd asked her to play her violin at one point but she was
   laughing too much to get the thing under her chin —
I thought this is going well . . .
But then she said she wanted to go home —
(2 and 3 of a three-gig visit yet to go) —
She'd sensed that the folk who'd booked me wondered what
   she was doing there —
('sensitive to what people are thinking and feeling') —
I said to hang on —
Second Night, they'd understand, because Second Night she
   would REALLY be in it —
How? What did I mean? —
Ahah! I said —
(because I didn't know) —
And could she cook a Vietnamese supper for all my
   Amsterdam chums at Dirk's place? —
She liked that idea and I gave her money to go shop the next
   day —
(And keep her out of my way while I thought what to
   do . . .) —
Second Night I shortened the Quantum Mechanics and then
   called her onto the stage with her violin —

'Just accompany whatever I say,' I said —
And I told the audience all about St Johns and the St Johns
   Affirmation —
(I'd never spoken to Thieu-Hoa of any of these matters) —
And about our meeting in the field . . .
On the Eighth Day . . .
(I thought, well, if she is truly the Affirmed Person she'll like
   it —
If she's not she won't —
And either way I win!) —
And she liked it —
And the Amsterdam audience liked it —
And the Vietnamese feast at Dirk's was a sensation! —
And that's the when and how of it —
How VIOLIN TIME was born —
and we carried on doing this snippet work-in-progress
   VIOLIN TIME as a treat after Quantum Rude
   Mechanicals —
When we got into the bigger venues, it turned out she was
   allergic to light —
we had to sit her in a puddle of darkness —
Other than that, it seemed to have a lot of promise —
Tea or Wha'? loved my weird books —
'Have you read them ALL?' —
'Not all' —
She decided to read the ones I hadn't got round to yet —
Milton William Cooper's *Behold A Pale Horse* I remember
   she went off with first —
then she seemed to go a bit cold on it all —
arriving late (but not too late to do it, usually)[67] —
and at the end of the shows she'd not talk to me but go off and
   meet other people —
If I took her out for a meal, she'd spend most of it chatting to
   others on her nubile phone —
I examined my Affirmation . . .
I thought, Well what this is is a sullen mood! —
I've got to be creative with it —

If I got us on at the National Theatre . . . ! —
I had an idea for a show Tea or Wha'? and I might do there —
I told her that in my mind I lived in St Johns, Newfound-
land —
'And you don't live in *Woolwich* really either, do you?' I
asked —
She was doodling spiraglic mazes which she does everywhere,
all the time, on anything —
I was right —
in her mind she lives where she was when she was uprooted at
six:
Haiphong, North Vietnam —
'What we'll do,' I said, 'is we'll send you over to my home, St
Johns —
and then I'll go to Haiphong in my Mellors and tea-cosy, and
I'll sit outside your old address, and wait for something to
happen —
and this will form the basis of a show —
some kind of Mystical Geography piece' —
She didn't look all that thrilled with the notion —
I thought, That's probably because she thinks I'm just
talking —
one of those geezers who just talk —
I said: 'I'm not just talking, I'm going to do it!' —
And I rang Richard Eyre at the National Theatre and got an
appointment.

III: *Inn of the New Temple by the Sea*

In which Richard Eyre possibly acts strange in a toilet; of Dodos, aliens and the Millennium, Human Genome Experimentation, reincarnation; a primordial Black Hole; a wedding; much laughter and several happy conclusions

It was a Linneker Day —
one of those days when I can't get my underpants right —
(named in fond memory of my old Maths master Roger
    Linneker
who couldn't keep his class or underpants in order) —
'That *Evening Standard* Award,' said Richard,
'was all Coveney's doing' —
'I know,' I said. 'Coveney and I were both in the same
    amateur dramatics company in Ilford all those years ago –
    the Ilford Renegades – so he always looks after me when he
    can – there's no money involved' —
'Well,' said Richard, 'you're in the worst predicament that can
    befall —
You are the victim of Famation of Character —
That show you did here before was OK —
but they didn't say it was OK —
they said it was brilliant – that you're a genius —
Is it your opinion that you're a genius?' —
'No,' I said —
'Well there you are then: Famation of Character —
They've got you on the hamster/gerbil treadwheel now —
it means that your next show has got to be better than they said
    your last one was —
Is there anywhere else you'd rather live than here?' —
'Yeah,' I said. 'St Johns, Newfoundland' —
'Go there – Stay there with these fine reviews,' says
    Richard —

'Then you will have won —
Your following (face it, not big) is dwindling to those who
   only come in the hope of monitoring your collapse —
Have you got any secret weaponry?' —
Me: 'Do you know what's called the Orificular Answer to
   Audience Restlessness?' —
'. . . no?' said Richard —
I've known about this for years —
Up on stage, we actors are all right because we get to move
   about —
but in the audience you're kinda stuck there —
after twenty minutes or so, your orifices start to concrete up a
   bit —
Up on stage, we can release some of the tension by subtly
   stressing one orifice after another —
For example, I've seen Sir Ian McKellan, whilst delivering a
   speech, back up against the corner of a table in the interests
   of relieving audience tension —
Ballet, for instance, would be boring if it weren't for that
   constant tension gained by the audience's subconscious
   concern that the male dancers are going to clout their
   bollocks on something —
Richard said: 'Well that's hardly orificular, is it?' —
'No,' I said. 'It's protuberential —
The subliminal rhythm of all successful theatre is
   Protuberance / Orifice —
The Protuberential / the Orificular —
A Demanding Protuberance / a Protesting Orifice —
or in Comedy: a Wilting Protuberance / a Snapping Orifice' —
'That's both amusing and profound,' said Richard —
'Do you know *Foucault's Pendulum*?'[68] —
'The scientific exhibit in the Conservatoire des Arts et Métiers
   in Paris? or Umberto Eco's book?' I asked —
'I was thinking of the book,' he said —
'Yes,' I said, 'I've read it five times —
I'm currently committing it to memory'[69] —
'Good Lord,' said Richard —

'Well, it's arguably the finest compendium of esoteric crap
    ever put together —
Why, what did you think of it?' —
'I didn't get past Chapter Two,' said Richard. 'Some of the
    words were a bit long for me' —
He went into the adjoining office and came back with an
    almost mint hardback edition —
He opened a page at random —
'What are proglottides?' he asked —
'Tapeworm segments' —
'Chelae?' —
'Crab, also scorpion, claws' —
'Macumba?'[70] —
'The snake-kissing Mormon cum Voodoo cult of Brazil (also
    found on Ivory Coast) which includes Russian Roulette in
    its Eucharist' —
'Potio-section?' —
'The art of slicing soup' —
'Tetraplyoctomy?' —
'Ability to split a hair down the middle into four —
that's when the heroes are planning their School of
    Comparative Irrelevance where useless or impossible
    courses are given —
The purpose of the School is to turn out scholars capable of
    endlessly increasing the number of unnecessary subjects,
    eventually leading to full comprehension of the underlying
    reasons for the Absurdity of Everything . . .
Have I passed?' —

Richard said I ought to write a concordance for *Foucault's
    Pendulum* —
I said: 'No – Umberto writes like that because it's potentially
    mind-damaging information he's dealing with, and it's to
    put the wankers off' —
Oops! —

Attempting to adjust my underpants and what I'd just said, I
    added:
'. . . But a concordance for very busy, highly intelligent,
    balanced people —
Yes – might be an idea' —
'Pee,' said Richard. 'Need a pee?' —
'No,' I said —
He nodded and winked —
I followed him out into what I used to think of as the
    'labyrinth' —

What was all this about? —
I was feeling light-headed. I started to gush:
'Let's hope we don't find any dimethoxyphenylathilomide in
    our wee' —
'Mmm,' said Richard —
'Dimethoxyphenylathilomide: the trace element found in the
    urine of all schizophrenics – in our tellurine flows' —
Richard stopped —
'Are tellurine flows the same as telluric currents?' —
'Yes – I was being funny' —
We were at the loo —
I followed Richard in —
He turned on all the taps of the wash-basins —
he turned on the showers and flushed all the loos, came up
    behind me and whispered in my ear:
'What primary school did you go to?' —
'Gearies,' I said —
'And what happened every day?' he said —
'I don't know,' I said —
'Milk,' he said —
'Yeah, that's right. Every day we had to drink a third of a pint
    of milk —
Take it in turns to be milk monitors —
The favourite job was donking the hole in the milk tops' —
'And then what happened?' —

'?' —

'Nurse and Doctor come to the school to see if you need your tonsils and adenoids out' —

'Yes! . . . ?' —

'There were crystals in the milk!' says Richard —

He went around flushing all the toilets again —

Apparently there were crystals in the milk so that they were able to tell the Neophobes from the Neophiles —

You know the world can be divided into two, don't you? —

The world can be divided into those who think the world can be divided into two, and those who don't. And of the former sort, one way of doing it is to divide it into the Neophobes (the loathers of things new) and the Neophiles[71] (the lovers of things new). According to Richard, the crystals (think of crystal sets here) lodge at the back of the brain. And they could diagnose Neophobes and Neophiles. Now maybe the odd Neophobe did actually need their tonsils and adenoids out. But *all* Neophiles *had to have theirs out!* And during the operation, a device was put in their head, cruder but similar to the device that the Queen's had put in her corgis so she knows where they are and what they're up to at all times[72] —

'Do you ever get ideas,' asked Richard, 'and you just don't know where they've come from?' —

'Yes,' I said. 'Often' —

'So do I,' said Richard. 'In the States they use a long thin spoon and shove it up the Neophiles' noses, right up, and go wooey-wooey in the frontal lobes. Have you never asked yourself WHY Americans don't appreciate irony? Why David Mamet can't finish his sentences? You could touch on these matters if we have you do another show here, but don't quote me because I'll have to deny it' —

'Of course,' I said, and helped him turn off all the taps and wotnot.

Had this happened?! —
(Back in the Grey Men's sad shot at a labyrinth) —
Was that really real? – Probably not. Probably some sick
  'virtual' scene broadcast into my implant.

Back in his office —
'So for reasons arcane you want to send some tart off to
  Newfoundland . . .' —
'She's not a tart!' I said. 'She's a classical violinist!' —
'Right,' he said. 'Whilst you go to sit outside an address in
  Haiphong in Disgraced Heritage Minister denture-wear and
  tea-cosy?' —
'Yes; for Geographically Mystical reasons – ' —
'You know David Mellor was very good to us?' said
  Richard —
'and it wasn't good news for us when he was disgraced and
  had to go' —
I said: 'These are absolute facsimile dentures —
they don't take the piss in any way . . .' —
'I've seen them,' said Richard —
He said: 'There's a lot about "tellurine flows" in *Foucault's
  Pendulum*, isn't there?' —
'Yes,' I said. 'Tellurine flows, telluric currents – they come in
  and out of the plot – there's no big chunk' —
'Mm,' he said. 'You couldn't mark up my book for all the
  tellurine references could you?' —
I said: 'Yeah, sure' —
'I think you should see Brenda,' he said —
Ah hah HAH! – smicker, snicker, smiggur, SNORKS! —
I'd won! I'd got commissioning money to fund the caper.

The money came through —
I sent Tea or Wha'? off to stay in St Johns —
in my home, actually: Ed Riche's spare room —
And to return, perhaps, as the Toast of St Johns —
fulfilling my Affirmation to the letter.

Ah! I couldn't wait for her return —
'How was it?' I said when she got back —
'Cold' —
I knew something was really wrong —
It turned out some of her friends had seen us performing —
You see, I'd thought we looked kinda charming together —
but no —
apparently it looked awful —
it looked like some awful old Kraut and a Bangkok bar girl —
Worse to tell you: she was a fifty-grand girl —
she was ripe and ready for marriage —
If you fell in love with her and if she fell in love with you, well
    that would be nice —
but then you would have to go and get the permission of her
    father —
and if he gave you the permission, you'd have to give him fifty
    grand! —
(That's the way they do things in Woolwich) —
and of course he's protected his investment by having her
    insured by Triad Woolwich Inc. —
Being seen with me will drop her value (it was possible she
    was only worth forty grand already!) —
and could result in me being cleaved in twain by her father's
    insurance company —
Was this the end of the line? —

I rang up Cathy and Mike:
'I think this affirmation business might be bollocks actually,
    Cathy' —
She said: 'We've all wrecked our lives over here with
    affirmations —
But we love you, so we thought you should have a go.'
(Cathy also told me she was pregnant —
by the abstemious Drinking Buddhist.)

A couple of days later I got a postcard:

'Dear Ken,' it said. 'The Dodo is not extinct. It currently resides on a lost atoll in the Indian Ocean, dreaming of revenge! Want to know more? Ring Gillian' and a Notting Hill Gate number —

I ring Gillian, and I'm talking to an Australian voice and I ask can we meet? —

She's got tickets to go to a John Pilger event at the ICA — film and chat about the miseries of East Timor —

Would I like to go to that? —

Yes, I would – Terrific.

And it turns out that Gillian is *five foot tall and a half-Javanese* Australian! —

'half-Charverknees' she pronounces it —

She's the illegitimate daughter of a Research Biologist of some renown and his Charverknees cook —

Crick and Watson's discovery of the DNA figure-of-8 thing was inspired (if not to some extent ripped off) from the notes of her father, who was so important when she was a kid she had to be followed everywhere 'cos of the fear that she might be kidnapped —

Her Dad was dead now —

and it wasn't suicide:

you can't strangle yourself and then sling yourself out of a window —

No – he was done in because of his objection to the public being kept in ignorance of the deal President Truman did with the aliens in 1947 —

insectoidal aliens incidentally —

not the funny slanty-eyed 'greys' of the Whitley Strieber books[73] —

(so don't get that muddled) —

Surely in my wide reading I'd come across the accounts of the crashed IAC? —

(IAC, note! Not UFO! IAC – Identified Alien Craft —

not ETs either, but EBEs – Extraterrestrial Biological
  Entities! —
Man, what a girl! She was thirty-three – *not old!*) —
Anyway, on board the crashed and Identified Alien Craft were
  human body parts —
No mucking about with these EBEs —
their technology is way superior to ours —
in fact, we are their property[74] —
we were bred by them for some purpose (we don't know quite
  what yet) —
but they're back now checking the stock —
And what's this business about the Dodo? —

And then she turns me on to this new way of talking:
'Old Map / New Map' —
Have you heard that before? —
It's 'millennium-speak' —
It turns out that everything's going to change on January 2nd,
  Twenty Hundred —
it's not going to be called the Year Two Thousand, but Twenty
  Hundred —
and January *2nd* (to give us the 1st to get over the Seeing in
  the Millennium Piss-up) . . .
You know like it was when we changed to decimal
  currency? —
It's gonna be like that, but quadra-cubed to the power of
  itself —
Everything I talk about in my shows, apparently, is what's
  called Old Map —
'Oh,' I said, 'so you come to my shows?' —
Yes, she's seen all of them —
more than once —
I realise I've seen her in my audiences —
(she radiates) —
Does she get comps? I ask —

Well no, but she doesn't pay because she monitors my shows
 for subversive content for the CIA —
after the tragic throttling and defenestration of her father, she
 got chatting to the folk who follow her around, and, having
 as much artistic bent as scientific, got offered this line of
 work —
She used to have to cover the whole of the British fringe —
but now she specialises in just me and Snoo Wilson —
'The Dodo?' —
Well everyone who knows anything is planning for the next
 millennium —
The Twentieth Century is just the last few miserable minutes
 on a clock —
and then the page will be turned —
We'll all walk into the terrific light of the Twenty-First
 Century.

At this moment a monument is about to be stuck up to all the
 recently extinct species: from the Dodo to today —
all the main ones we're responsible for —
the artwork is terrific, with the Dodo at the bottom —
and it's going to fanfare round the major cities of the world,
draped whenever possible in the AIDS Quilt —
Only thing holding it up is that the design's got the Wild Tiger
 on the top and there's still a few of the buggers hanging
 on —
But they should be gone by the end of the summer —
and then we can get touring this splendid *guilt* and *misery*
 piece to see out the millennium —

But then on January 2nd, Twenty Hundred —
they're all going to start coming back —
By the method popularised in *Jurassic Park* —
All those species are going to start coming back, starting with
 the Dodo —

and we've already got that one, hiding on that atoll in the
   Indian Ocean —
And Jupiter! 310 times the size, weight and mass of Earth —
and orbiting Jupiter at this moment is the Rocket Galileo —
on board a payload of 47.9 pounds of plutonium and timed for
   the concluding seconds of December 1999 it's going to
   cease orbiting and plunge into Jupiter —
plutonium will set off a chain reaction converting Jupiter into
   a star, in the process heaving out loads of stuff which should
   include several eventually habitable planets —
On January 2nd Twenty Hundred they'll come clean about the
   manned space stations on the moon and Mars —
How could I have imagined that having got there umpteen
   years ago we haven't kept going back and back and got
   things more than a little bit sorted? – helped in the project
   considerably (says Gillian) by Truman's EBEs —

Can we trust these insectoidal EBEs? —
Yes, she says, we can – in the sense that the chicken trusts the
   farmer —

And on January 2nd Twenty Hundred the cure for most
   cancers and the cure for AIDS, and out in the open we can
   run cars on water —
We've got all this already, but better to wait and use them to
   dramatise the wonder and joy of the New Millennium and
   the New World Order —
the entire population to be DNA profiled —
all toilets will automatically test all URINE and FÆCAL
   MATTER and send data by modem to the BEAST —
The BEAST not only likes to know where you are,
he likes to know *how* you are! —

What a lady! —

and why are you telling me all this? *and do you play the violin?* —

'The violin? I don't. But *Ah do*' —

and when she says 'Ah do' she says it in a different voice —

a kind of weird French accent:

'I don't. But *Ah do*' —

What? —

'And why am I telling you this? Because, you arse, it was *me* you affirmed in, not that Vietnamese cuckoo' —

Cuckoo? —

She's now lecturing me on the breeding habits of the cuckoo —

The cuckoo doesn't bother building a nest —

it spies on meadow peewits, lets them build a nest, lay half a doz eggs in it, then nips in, kicks out one of the eggs and lays one of its own, which look just like little peewit eggs —

peewit eggs take fourteen days to hatch out, but cuckoo eggs *only thirteen and a half* —

and the newborn cuckoo is a *natural born ovicidal maniac* —

As soon as it's out of its shell, it humps all the other eggs out of the nest —

And then the cuckoo grows fast and enormous, six times bigger than its half-wit peewit foster Mum and Dad who race about feeding the awful thing —

Evidently I've been a foolish peewit flying around, going blue-arsed for Tea or Wha'? the cuckoo —

she happened to be in a field —

that's where you find cuckoos: in fields —

My Affirmation should have led me to her – Gillian —

she to be my comedy partner —

With the material she could supply, clearly a sensation would be automatic — .

and the plan? —

that I should MC in the Millennium —

I'd've become by that time some sort of Intergalactic
    Buddha —
and I'd see us into all the wonders, as Jupiter blows up and so
    on —
World-wide, satellite, TV, InterNet hook-up —
And, she said, Murielle agreed —
? —
In fact it was Murielle's idea —
? —
Murielle? —
Well – apparently Gillian was not only Gillian —
she was also Murielle —
and Murielle wasn't only Murielle, she was in fact a
    reincarnation of a thirteenth-century Heretic Lady by the
    name of Esclarimonde . . .

What is the date of my Affirmation? she wants to know —
I don't know off-hand —
She suggests it's 3rd October, 1994 —
(She was right) —
And what, she asks me, happened that day? —
Dunno —
Answer: Alpine Armaggedon —
Dr Luc Jouret and his financial sidekick di Mambro and their
    Cult of Death remove themselves and their flock from
    Montreal to Switzerland —
(Montreal having been founded by Cathar heretics – did I not
    know that?
Actually, I did) —
Cathars into reincarnation *under will* —
Tracing their incarnations back to long before Christ —
And they went to Switzerland to seed the coming new
    Millennium —
to ready it for the joy of overt Cathar takeover —

and to do this by shuffling off their present mortal coil and
   immediately possessing or par-possessing key-figures in the
   Pyramid of Power, plus others who would be useful in their
   endeavour —
And when the bag went up in Switzerland, Murielle[75] stroke
   Esclarimonde (one of Luc Jouret's crew) made a bee-line
   for Gillian —
and the three now shared the Gillian body —

'I don't. But *Ah do*' —
Gillian meant by this that *she* couldn't play the violin, but
   Esclarimonde could, (as long as the thing was strung
   according to medieval principle) —
And Esclarimonde / Murielle had par-possessed Gillian at the
   very moment I'd been tricked into asserting that my
   affirmee (Gillian) *had to play the violin* —
and where was I at the time? —
Newfoundland – first port of call of the fleeing Cathars! —
I said: Why did Jouret and his gang go to Switzerland to
   burn? —
'CERN.'
Hmm.

Another member of Jouret's troop was Joël Lerendu —
Gillian tells me that Lerendu was a reincarnation of the
   thirteenth-century Minstrel / Troubadour heretic Norman
   'Le Croc' de Dijon —
Norman had been involved with Esclarimonde back in the
   thirteenth century, and likewise as Lerendu with Murielle in
   the twentieth —
and in his recent reincarnation he'd seen me perform at the
   Longshoremen's Protective Union Hall in St Johns —
Also Luc and Jo had read the account of my JEST idea in the
   in-house est mag, and attempted a humour workshop and
   Booger with the flock before nipping off to buy the
   petrol —

And Joël had intended to make for and par-possess me when
the bag went up, but in the last few days he's started to
dicker a bit and wonder if maybe David Icke wasn't a better
bet —
Murielle / Esclarimonde were against this,
mainly because they didn't like David's taste in jerseys —
Now was the question: What had happened to Norman? —
Had I not let him in? —
maybe some malfunctioning in my Richard Eyre Milk
Implant? —
Gillian / Murielle / Esclarimonde had approached David Icke
on this —
He was now wearing frilly shirts for his gigs, so maybe Joël
was in there . . .
But Icke had been unforthcoming . . . 'cagey' —
Maybe Joël had split off to Icke and Norman had come to
me? —
But was still out in the cold? —

Gillian had done a great meal: spiced squid in a nest of
marinated noodles —
She said: 'I love you, and you affirmed me – so that's
sweet' —
But it's not going to work, apparently, unless I allow in par-
possession by Norman and Joël for the sake of Murielle and
Esclarimonde —
'How cosy that'd be: a *ménage à six*' – (or *cinq* if J had split to
I) —
'Mmm . . .' I said —

There's a way of arsing around with the gene of a certain jelly-
fish and grass so you get a luminous lawn —
Airfields will all be sown with it ready for Spring Twenty
Hundred —
Midnight Cricket will also benefit.

She told me about the Human Genome Experiment —

Crick of Crick and Watson, the DNA blokes, was taking one of her father's ideas farther —

Apparently you just have to arse around a bit with a couple of links in the human DNA and you can double the human brain, not in size, but in interconnections – this will square, possibly cube, its thinking and deductive powers —

'Be a bit like Stephen Hawking . . .' I said —

'Ah,' says Gillian, 'it'd be way beyond Sadie' —

('Sadie Hawkings' is apparently the way 'in' people refer to the Great Man)[76] —

Anyway: Would I be up to fathering such a child? she wants to know —

'Hmmm . . .' —

Gillian says to have a think about it – she has the contacts.

And she gave me what you might call a 'Medical Yogurt Pot' with the instruction that, if I ever found myself up to it, to put my contribution immediately into the freezer and arrange for rapid collection —

In any event, Esclarimonde wanted me to go off to the Pair o' Knees —

(? —

Ah! The *Pyrénées* – Cathar Country) —

in the hope that there I might let in Norman 'Le Croc' de Dijon —

The Pyrénées . . .

Mmm . . . I was thinking the next morning —

Do I really need to go there? —

The phone rang: it was Tea or Wha'? —

She was short of money – had I got any jobs? —

she wouldn't actually mind doing shows with me – ? —

She sounded very merry on the phone —

She was going back to Newfoundland —

she'd felt 'called' —

she wanted to know if I'd been yet to Haiphong in my teeth —

I said I hadn't, but of course I would be —

I thought, I haven't got the money to go to the Pyrénées AND
  Haiphong —
and I thought about Tea or Wha'? —
Had I really gone to the End of the Line on that? —
No I hadn't, because I hadn't gone to Haiphong in my
  Mellors —
So: Go to the Pyrénées with the intention of getting
  possessed —
or —
Go to the Port of Haiphong in Tea-cosy and Mellors? —
Not an everyday decision . . .
The Universe shall decide —
I took out a coin: Head Haiphong; tails Pyrénées —
Heads —
I packed cosy and teeth . . . and went to the Pyrénées!
'Why have you come here?' said the waiter in the restaurant at
  Montségur as I leafed through the Arthur Guirdham books
  he'd brought me —
I said: 'I've come to see if I can get par-possessed by Joël
  Lerendu (if Icke's not got him), one of Dr Luc Jouret's
  Montreal Cathar Death Brigade, who was, more
  importantly, himself a reincarnation of Norman 'Le Croc'
  de Dijon of the thirteenth century; if I'm successful in
  allowing him entry, I may then, if I wish, if Joël and
  Norman agree, wank into a Medical Yogurt Pot which will
  then be scurried, in pomp, from my freezer (I guess in some
  kind of thermos) to Crick the Nobel Prizewinner's place
  where he will genetically arse around with it, eventually
  fertilising a half-Charverknees Australian whose father was
  strangled and defenestrated due to a difference of opinion
  over Insectoidal Aliens whom President Truman had
  befriended back in 1947; the Charverknees/Australian lady
  who monitors my performances for subversive elements for
  the CIA (not just mine, Snoo Wilson's as well; Snoo – an
  unusual name but easy to remember because spelled
  backwards it's 'oons', an expression used frequently in
  comedies of the Restoration period – is par-possessed by

Murielle, who is a reincarnation of Esclarimonde). It's part
of the Human Genome Experiment, and our offspring will
have a good chance of enhanced brain circuitry, possibly
cubing the performance of Sadie Hawkings —
There's a lot more I could tell you, but I'm not sure it would
mean a lot to you unless you've at least a nodding
acquaintance with the negative nesting habit of cuckoos' —
'Esclarmonde[77] de Fanjeaux?' said the waiter —
'I think so,' I said —
'We had an Esclarmonde staying in the guest-house last
week' —
'I guess they can't all be Esclarmonde . . .' I said —
'Why not?' said the waiter. 'In Melbourne I worked for a bit in
the Loony Bin. We had two Cleopatras – and they didn't
fight —
they had so much in common —
There are so many more people in the world now —
maybe that's why there's so much less full reincarnation, and
more and more par-possession these days. They have to
kinda spread themselves —
a sort of time-share arrangement' —
'Are you par-possessed?' I asked —
He shook his head —
But that was for the benefit of the old man on the other
table —
because on my serviette he wrote: 'OC' —
I said quietly: 'If I get par-possessed, will I know?' —
'You will know if you want to know – if you Gnow what I
mean . . .' —

The old gentleman on the next table called me over —
He was English —
'From Bath?' —
'No-o,' he said —
I knew I knew him – from something . . .
Who is he. . . ? Something was missing . . .

HIS NAME TAG!!! —
'JACK !'

Shortly after Erhard's est, Jack had discovered he was a
    reincarnation of Evangeline,[78] a thirteenth-century
    heretic —
In the Montségur bonfire, Evangeline sadly hadn't managed
    the Last Laugh from the blaze —
Jack pointed up Mount Montségur —
'What do you think they were doing up there for that two
    weeks of the truce? To be able to come down from the
    mountain like a Works Outing from the Ministry of Funny
    Walks, singing Rugby Songs six centuries before the
    invention of Rugby, and then jump laughing and hooting
    into the bonfire? —
Answer: JEST Humour Workshops, in essence – Bogomil or
    Booger Events certainly' —
'But you didn't come on my JEST,' I said —
'No,' he said, 'but I sent my sister . . .' —
'FAT ARSE!' I said —
'Fat Arse,' said Jack, 'or Sarah, as I more usually called her
    . . . She was marvellously changed after your JEST –
    became a loved headmistress of a Surrey Girls' Boarding
    School – got par-possessed by Roger of Carcassonne, and
    wound up setting light to herself in front of the sixth form
    (the science set, I think), laughing wonderfully from the
    blaze – The *News of the World* headlined it: "CACKLE
    CRACKLE!" – Sarah. She had a good end, bless her!' —
He said: 'That's why we're interested in you, Kenneth —
to run JEST Humour Workshops for Reincarnating Death
    Cults' —
'Like Jouret's?' I said —
'Exactly,' he said. 'Give us a good end —
A designated Bathroom Break, I think. I want to show you
    something . . .'

I followed Jack into the Hommes —
He undid his belt and dropped his trousers,
in kind of cowboy-cum-flamenco style —
'To make Evangeline feel at home, I had myself fixed up with
    female regalia,' said Jack, showing me his lack of *thing* —
'Works OK if I keep it oiled,' he said. Adding:
'Didn't bother with the tits.'
(Thought of as a woman he wasn't utterly unattractive —
You know when they've had enough of you in Hampstead
    Pubs and they ring that number and the fat policewoman
    comes round and sits on your head? —
Kind of like her) —

'I have some control over it, which was unexpected,' said
    Jack —
and he flexed some recently re-routed muscles —
and it was . . . *weird* . . . it appeared to be singing . . . or
    miming, perhaps, to some ditty lodged somehow in Jack's
    Italian Arse-brain —
The performance went on long enough for me to have worked
    out the words had I the lip-reading ability —

'More wine!' said Jack, suddenly, pulling up his trousers —
On the way back to the table, he took a violin off the wall and
    played a quick jig, Newfoundland style, from the hip —
'Norman is knocking, Ken . . . let him in' —

Weird goings-on in the lav made me think of Richard Eyre —
'What's all the interest in Tellurine these days?' I asked
    Jack —
Apparently Truman's EBEs[79] are sending a baby Black Hole
    our way (just a primordial littl'un: the mass of the moon and
    a Schwarzschild Radius of a mere ten thousandth of an
    inch) —
due early Twenty Hundreds, it's headed for Bosnia,

guided in by the CERN Sausage —
as it comes in, the land and stuff'll go up to meet it like
    'magnetised jello'
and then hurtle back down with the Black Hole into the Earth
    and out the other side —
somewhere between New Zealand and Santiago —
and then off to blast the moon apart —
(the moon'll reassemble eventually, but be red and molten for
    years) —
(more data for my Intergalactic Buddha entertain-
    ments . . .) —
The Baby Black Hole will charge up the Earth's telluric
    currents —
the fault lines —
the vortices —
THE LINES OF SYNCHRONOS! —
and Standing Stones: cromlechs, menhirs, Stonehenges, and
    Aveburys —
any that are still correctly marking telluric anomalies'll pung
    and blast up out of their sitings —
(not into orbit, but fucking high) —

After that, the economy's not going to be a Black Economy,
but a Black Hole Economy —
and that's why tellurine knowledge is at a premium —
only the telluric can tell us our future.

In his Black Ops days, Jack worked with the guy Donald
    Sutherland played in *JFK* —
(guy calls himself 'X' in the film but his real name's Prouty or
    Bunty or something) —
Jack, Bunty and a whole team of castratory euphorics are
    going to be there at magnetised jello time when they and
    most of what was Yugoslavia rises up, then swirls down
    forming an intra-global drinking straw, and then shooting
    off for lunar destruct —

'So we want you to give us a highly-paid, top class JEST
   Humour Workshop and Booger Event before we transit —
A Good End,' says Jack —
'The Best End that's ever been offered since the dawning of
   man . . .' —

'Hmm. Interesting gig, Jack,' I said.
'I nearly didn't come here, you know —
I was going to Haiphong —
in Mellors and tea-cosy' —
I showed him.
Jack became serious:
'Norman!' he said —

And it's the next day —
And I'm below in the Bookshop —
Wall to wall Heresy! —
'Brûlez Cathares! Brûlez!' —
Terrific.

So I'd got my pile of comics —
Chants de Pyrène Vols. 1, 2, 3 and 4 —
and I'd found the 'Song of the Fotedor' in *Burlesque et
   obscénité chez les troubadours* —
I was disappointed that it was attributed to either Anonyme or
   Tribolet and not Norman 'Le Croc' de Dijon —
but I'd put it on the pile . . .
and then I came across this: *Clowns of the Free Spirit* by
   Herbert J. Wimple[80] (the cover slightly burned) —
in which:

YOU'RE NOT LOOKING WELL, DEAR!
There were many 'Tribolet's of which the best loved was
Norman 'Le Croc' de Dijon, comedy minstrel/troubadour
(1181?–1244). The 'Croc' refers not to his crocodile mouth
(although he had one – he was an 'onky', 'un homme qui

rit', with cut mouth) but to his FINGER[81] which was his main and very versatile comedy prop, a forerunner of Chaplin's cane and the cigar of W. C. Fields. Norman was also a funeral undertaker, and in the thirteenth century, the mortician was expected to give the corpse periodic pokes with his index finger or 'croc' to give it some last opportunities to exhibit life.

It was said that Norman's comedy routines were a spur to longevity: with his catchphrase, 'You're not looking well, dear!' said with concern, but counterpointed by the hilariously obscene antics of his seemingly uncontrollable 'croc', an alarming little being with its own triple-jointed agenda, 'the fear of what he was going to get up to with you once you were dead caused you to put off the day of your demise for as long as possible.'
(DIED SIEGE OF MONTSÉGUR, 1244.)

In the Langue d'Oc
The meaning of 'croc'
Is the Undertaker's digit,
With which he pokes
Dead girls and blokes
To give 'em a last chance to fidget;

'Le Croc' Norm, his finger . . .
Can en-quire . . . and linger . . .
Such that if you have any feeling,
With what he will do
You will find that you
Have to be scraped off the ceiling.

And then SHE comes in —
With her pulled-back hair and shorts —
Goes straight to my pile of books —
pulls out Vol. 2 of *Les Chants de Pyrène* —
'Non! C'est mon colomne de livres que je veux acheter!' —

'Pfffff —' (that rude blowing thing that French girls do[82]) —
I snap her in the shop —
The snap outside —
She drives off —
My plans . . .
And that's when Norman comes in!! —
And he came in through my finger!!! —
NORMAN: 'Which way she go?' —
'Dunno! That way!' —
'Fot!' —
We bought a case of fine wines, and before the end of the sixth
bottle had composed this poem:

> It was for sure at Montségur (where heretic bods were
>   burned)
> That a lady fair with pulled-back hair my pleadings mocked
>   and spurned.
> She posed for the click of my camera's pic with a laughing,
>   mocking look –
> And I loathed her, yes, but I loved her as her arms
>   embraced my book.
>
> You only love the things that fade
> That go and won't come back
> And LOVE, FAITH, HOPE and CHARITY
> Are ferrets in a sack.
>
> O! ring the bell of the Cathar's hell, which is the here and
>   now;
> For everything we feel, hear, see – the Devil takes his bow:
> He makes us turn and never learn and sends us back to
>   'Start',
> 'N' with motives heinous gets Gleeful Meanness to open up
>   our heart!
>
> And as she left me quite bereft of Number Two in my set
> With her laugh unkind and her pert behind – I made a kinda
>   bet:
> 'I bet this mo so small and so insignif in your life's

> adventure
> Will grizzly be as I busily be, and'll come to ever haunt yer.'

I had the pic blown huge and big and hung it outside my
  house;
Fashion dummies, a score (in fact slightly more) I bought
  off a jolly Scouse,
And in my lair I pulled their hair back and dressed them all
  in shorts
And I stuck them out and round about and I wound up in the
  Courts.

''Twas an act born of a love forlorn, your honour, 'tis true
  – a fact:
The defendant let a mental bet, spored by a mean, mean
  act,
To say: "Hell no! That moment won't go!" – and hatch out
  this plan to catch
The Press's attention and, ultimately, a mention, and her
  pic in the Paris Match.'

I'd met the beak the previous week, quite late, in a sordid
  club.
He swallowed my story and even more, he ably expressed
  the nub:
'This man – who nicked him!? – is clearly the victim of love
  in most loathsome form –
He shouldn't be here! Let's give him a cheer! O! were his
  courage the norm!'

And look! – [Pointing at huge painted blow-up of the
  photo of the Lady from Montségur]
She's there! With pulled-back hair, posing in Montségur
  Lane!
And we're betting, up there as setting, it'll jog a seeker's
  brain.
And once she's snared, and pert bum bared, and whips are
  raised and must
Norman and I will wink the eye and turn aside from LUST.

You only love the things that fade
That go and won't come back
And LOVE, FAITH, HOPE and CHARITY
Are ferrets in a sack:

Here is FAITH, a polecat cross –
She knows she'll catch a rabbit;
And CHARITY, he knows it too –
He also knows he'll nab it!

But leave a bit for FAITH to eat,
And a few bones for HOPE . . .
But for LOVE he don't know what to do;
With LOVE he can't quite cope.

Seeker! Of ferret LOVE beware!
It has the keenest bite;
You can't just stick it down your pants –
It must be handled right.

'The Lady from Montségur' —
(Norman was definitely 'in' now – now I gnew what it's like
    to gnow something) —
Soon as we got back, we went out to get dummies —
they're not cheap —
any decent secondhand ones get snapped up by the rigs.
Gillian came round as Norman and I were arsing around
    getting shorts up a dummy —
Gillian assumed this was some sort of antic towards her
    Yoghurt Pot Project —
I said: 'O yes, I was all go on that, but then I got a
    headache' —
'Just lie back and think of Newfoundland,' says Gillian —
Norman muttered to me: 'She's the same kinda pain she was
    centuries ago' —
But we let her get on —

And then, phoning for a cab, holding receptacle aloft like a
    trophy, she says:
'This marks the turning point in human evolution!'

It's interesting how you get shorts on one of these —
One leg slots into the other —
(gives you an insight into life on a rig) —

Since I haven't got a SELF – merely a 'seating' – I'm
    available for Norman's use —
20 kilometres from Damanhur, near where they filmed *The
    Name of the Rose*,
Norman took me to an ancient standing stone —
23 paces nor'-nor'-east of the thing, he had me dig —
and we unearthed a buckle he had buried there in the early
    1200s —
unquestionably his – the prodding bit that goes through the
    leather hole being a comically enquiring finger —
We reburied it, to be used as a sign or credential in some
    future century.
Apparently it was Norman who escaped out the back of
    Montségur —
(that's why they cut all their mouths to pose as him – to cover
    his absence —
they needed the two weeks for the wounds to heal) —
Anyway, Norman escaped out the back with the Holy Grail
    and brought the Grail to Newfoundland[83] —
sailing under Skull and Crossbones —
(The Skull and Crossbones was Norman's original coat-of-
    arms which he used for both his comedy and chain of
    Pyrenean Funeral Parlours) —
Up on the rocks at the edge of St Johns Harbour, on what's
    called now the Battery,
there was Norman's last home.[84]
The Holy Grail is the recipe for Humour —

Ken Dodd has a copy locked in a bank vault with his love
    letters —
dictated to him by Norman in that space between heartbeats
    when he crashed his bike as a kid and knocked his teeth into
    the shape we love them.

Thieu-Hoa came round with handsome Christopher
    Darlington[85] —
On her last night in Newfoundland they'd found each other —
Newfoundloves of Newfoundland —
She was going to move there and they were going to open a
    Musical Caff —
and they'd got me a booking to do *Violin Time* in the
    Longshoremen's Protective Union Hall in July, and they
    wondered if it would be OK to get married actually on the
    show? —
I said of course.
They were brimming with what this Caff was going to be
    like —
'Cos she's a great cook is Tiddley Pud —
Her pancake rolls and all —
Mind, you wouldn't want everything —
I imagine this scene:
It's your first time in the Caff —
you never were in such a place —
(no regular Caff, Mrs Darlington's) —
I expect you'll be admiring the (almost) complete collection of
    Philip K. Dick books which I donated —
(and the bloody nearly full set of *Fortean Times*es[86] right back
    to when it was called 'The News' (them was me as
    well)) —
Innocently you order Spesh of the Day: Chân gà râ'm —
arrives marinated chickens' feet —
(You'd been brung up nice and know that properly hens' feet
    are snipped from the carcase and then put in the bin) —
You wonder can you cope? —

You don't want to upset Mrs D because she's very pretty . . .
Could you pocket them? —
(they're bloated with many nights' marination) —
there are no paper serviettes —
(nor no knives and forks nor chopsticks, and if you ask can
    you have some, Mrs D says 'No' —
the form is, you trough in, and then wash up in the fine,
    communal, turn-of-the-century sink —
If you bring your own set of cutlery, Mrs Darlington doesn't
    fuss —
but don't, because you won't feel 'in' –) —
You're getting out your hanky in which to wrap the bulboid
    feet —
and then aware that Mrs D is at your table —
violin at the hip —
and she plays you 'Music of the Trees' —
so beautifully —
until you've eaten everything up like a good boy, and by then
    (and where did THEY come from?) Mrs Darlington has
    been joined by Flute, Bass and Banjo —
And you can't wait to introduce your mates to this
    gastronomical musical sensation.
Its name . . . ?
'The Café of Laughter and Forgetting'? —
NO! —
'The Caff of Laughter and REMEMBERING' —
where everything that has ever happened anywhere ever is
    now FUNNY! —
Yeah! except neither of those names 'cos both are poncey! —
But THAT the controlling idea of the Caff – yeah! —

The reason I know so much about how this Caff is going to be
    is I was with them when they took pen to paper and . . .
See, they haven't finally got the premises yet —
But this, at the moment of writing, is only the third day of their
    Caffirmation . . .

'Coming into our lives now is a Caff . . .' —
It was a Laffirmation putting it together! —
No, there was no way, no other way, that Tea or Wha'?
   wanted to live out her remaining eleven years till she had to
   snuff it in 2007. (The more than two fortune tellers had been
   very clear on this point.)

I thought: 'We've got to do something about that . . .' —
Norman said why not pack her off to Damanhur —
let her empty out her 'suitcase' there and maybe find there are
   one or two items she could do without for the rest of her
   journey —
maybe pick up some things there . . . ? —
I rang up Oberto to see if he could lay on some alchemical
   spiraglic do in the Temple of Mankind —
which might hack into her mainframe and destroy her deadly
   data —
I said: 'I'm sure she'd do a concert with the trees if you want
   her to . . .
in fact, she was a tree in a previous life, but not, she thinks, on
   this planet – ' —
ESPERIDE: 'Oberto's asking does she know which planet?' —
I said no I don't think so, 'I think it's just a kind of notion she
   has' —
ESPERIDE: 'Please send your friend. A happy outcome is
   possible.'
And so that was my wedding present —
The Gift of Longevity —
(I didn't want to be responsible for a Newf marrying a
   duff'n'.)

When it's her birthday now, she has to have three cakes, and
   they MUST be made by others —
a surprise till they arrive —
Remember that please Newfs! —
and then she won't be taken away! —

Cake One with candles to the number of years she is . . .
blow them out —
Cake Two with thirty-six candles . . .
these she has to blow out looking mature —
and then one with seventy or so . . .
which she blows out, tottering about —
she'll be good at that —
she gets it from her Mum who does terrific impressions of
    cripples —
was famous for them in old Haiphong.[87]

I recommend that Musical Caff —
downtown St Johns —
Opens in December —
It'll be in one of those descending alleys of steps between
    Duckworth and Water Street —
(ask in the Ship Inn –) —
And it will be there for a long time to come.

Having her 'suitcase' professionally repacked hasn't
    dampened Tea or Wha'?'s humour any —
in fact it's enhanced it —
but sometimes she looks at you not full on as she used to, but
    from her confidant periphery —
(and shit! will that be exciting for you as you yank a bit of
    duck web from your teeth and call for another toon from the
    Rubber Plant –) —
And this time next year we'll all look back and say:
'Well she sure BLOOMED on this planet!'[88]

Norman advises holding fire on final acceptance of Jack's
    lucrative offer of the Bosnian JEST workshop —
To offer our services to Oberto and Damanhur might be the
    better option —
Oberto's spiraglics might well divert the Black Hole . . .

Oberto's a Parfait, whereas Jack is merely well-intentioned.
What of Gillian, last seen taking off in a cab with thermos?
Haven't seen anything of her —
She's gone away —
I guess she's at Crick's —
What of the progeny? —
Will it be The Beast? —
Dunno.
We await data[89] —
ask in the Ship Inn or the Musical Caff – they'll have the news
   first.

Sometimes I don long-johns —
pad out —
and in Cosy and Mellors give myself over to Norman
   completely —
And then, scarcely myself present at all:
I am at my happiest.
As we await the process of this show:
to bring about the final piece of the jigsaw —
entrée of La Femme de Montségur.
And if it doesn't? —
Thieu-Hoa's Mum has promised to take me and Norman to
   Vietnam —
and there, outside a certain house, abandoned sixteen years
   ago in great haste,
in the Port of Haiphong —
she will surely show up.

And then maybe the three of us, Norm and Me (only costs us
   one ticket – the ideal Comedy Partner) plus Whatever Her
   Name Turns Out To Be —
(previously, centuries ago it was Floralmonde, wasn't it,
   Norman?) —
will be coming down the steps from a Canadian Airlines
   plane —

we'll hail us an off-licence —
and be, at last, HOME —
to be found, I suspect, most often, eating, carousing, and
   DANCING too – (!) —
WITH THE LISTENING-IN CONVERSATIONS FOR
   POSSIBILITIES! —
'What that mean?' —
'I don't know, Norman. I've never known —
It's a slice of a pie called never known and never will' —
'It's terrific!' —
'It is, isn't it' —
– in Mrs Darlington's[90] Musical Caff, St Johns Harbour: —
Turn left off the cold, sounding sea.

END[91]

Notes

1 Clarendon Press, Oxford.

2 *The Secret Life of Plants* by Peter Tompkins and Christopher Bird (Harper and Row, New York, 1973). See also Lyall Watson's *Supernature* (Hodder and Stoughton, 1973), pp. 247–248.

3 See note 26a below for details.

4 Before we go any further, get this book by close chum and seeker Jeff Merrifield: *The Perfect Heretics*. Available from: Playback, 9 Malden Road, Great Totham, Essex CM9 8PR. It opens: 'PREFACE: I first encountered the Cathars when a friend lent me a book. The friend: Ken Campbell . . . The book: *Flicker*.'[a]

    [a] *Flicker* (*Sunset Boulevard* meets *The Name of the Rose*) by Theodore Roszak (Bantam; ISBN 0553–40480–6).

5 In recent *Paris Match*, pics of di Mambro in front of the Great Pyramid of Cheops – good-looking, stocky; tash, shades; standing between his beautiful wife Jocelyne, and his equally lovely mistress Dominique – they both are scheduled for incineration. On another page, the di Mambros' little lad Elie in white robe holding rose. *Brûle Elie aussi.*

6 My favourite entire chapter of all books I have ever read is Chapter 10 of *Foucault's Pendulum*[a] by Umberto Eco in which is argued that there are only four classes of human being: 'Cretins, fools, morons and lunatics . . . The lunatic doesn't concern himself at all with logic; he works by short circuits. For him, everything proves everything . . . You can tell him by the liberties he takes with common sense, by his flashes of inspiration, and by the fact that sooner or later he brings up the Templars.'

    [a] Published by Picador (Pan Books Ltd), 1990. See also pages 90–91 of current text.

7 *Le 54e* by Thierry Huguenin (Editions Fixot, 1995; ISBN 2–221–08045–9).[a]

    [a] Norman's helping me through it. We're up to p. 142 – it's VERY good.

8 *Sunday Times* News Review, 'Insight', October 1994: '. . . Cathars, a thirteenth-century sect whose members burned themselves alive . . .' I

have nowhere else heard or read that they burned *themselves*. They were burned by the Inquisition. Unless this refers to their bravado jumping into the bonfires as narrated later . . .

9 Coveney. See also note 21[c3] and p. 89 of current text.

10 Today it's easy for us to see that, but they worked it out without the nightly help of Jeremy Paxman. I am not knocking the man, although it is sad to see how little he's unlearned since leaving university. (Did he ever win the de Montfort prize for anything?) But we've all got a bit of Jeremy Paxman in us. It's just he is a wee bit over requirement. Have a Good End, Jeremy.

11 I am particularly indebted to the anonymous seeker who sent me *RABELAIS, his life, the story told by him, selections therefrom here newly translated, and an interpretation of his genius and his religion* by John Cowper Powys (Village Press, 1974); and who has had the fine grace not to ask for it back.

12 Serie Moyen Age, dirigée par Danielle Regnier-Bohler, édition bilingue présentée par Pierre Bec.

13 See Scotland for similar aberration.

14 'To fuck with an inventiveness of orifice', Jeff Merrifield prefers. (As a translation.) It was the Cathar method of family planning. If your lover can relieve his tensions in your armpit we won't get saddled with a brat.

15 The upper lip is snipped and the mouth surgically extended E to W. When the thus facially modified owner attempts to 'keep a straight face' the result is automatically amusing. The late Tommy Cooper was almost naturally so endowed.

16 You find it in a book called *The Nag Hammadi Library*. Sadly in my version (E.J. Brill, Leiden, 1984) the translators (Members of the Coptic Gnostic Library Project of the Institute for Antiquity and Christianity) are a bit feeble with the comedy material. They seem to take a delight in unspringing the rhythm of the gags. Indeed, often they don't seem to have 'got it'. Worth having your own copy though, Seekers! Lots of other good stuff in it. E.g. The Gospel of Philip, who says the Virgin Birth is balls and misses the point entirely. (My translation.) A vital volume for when the Jehovah's Witness calls. Never waste a Jehovah's Witness!

17 Bookshop: Georges Servus, Montségur. The comic: *Rennes-le-Château, Le Secret de l'Abbé Saunière*. Textes et dessins par Antoine Captier, Marcel Captier, Michel Marrot. Belisane.

18 Number Two, I think. I'd give you all the blah, but I don't know what I've done with it. I've taken all my stuff out of boxes to make my place like Marvin Minsky's and I don't know my way round yet. FOUND IT! I'd put it in a special place I now remember so I wouldn't forget where it was. It's *Gnosis* 4 (PO Box 14217, San Francisco, CA 94110). Recent iss. on Solar Templars also good.

19 Times Books. It gives the Touring Circuit under 'Critics of Crusading', marking the Comedy Venues with HARPS!

20 Possible lexilink, Seekers? – Morin Heights, Quebec, was where the very first Solar Templars combusted, I've just noticed in Professor Robert O'Driscoll and Elizabeth Elliott's (he's quite old; she's quite a dish) *Corruption in Canada* (Saigon Press, Toronto, 1994, ISBN 0–921745–15–X). Seeker! Invite me not round to your squat or box unless you can at least give good reason for not owning this fat Cracker. Last I heard, Robert was banned from the University of Toronto for having published this.

21 Youthful James Nye, who's kindly (but for money) typing all this into his processor for me, rings to say excellent account of Moirans in current edition (No. 87) of *Fortean Times*. ' "Fire in the mountains: Experts of every stripe descended in January on Moirans-en-Montagne in the Jura mountains, France's toy-making capital, to investigate a mysterious 'combustion wave'. The trouble began on 4 November 1995, when Jean-Pierre Raffin's house in the rue de Cares burst into flames. At least sixteen fires followed, in five different houses, all in the afternoon and all but four on a Saturday. Tins, garden furniture and cement bags ignited without apparent cause. The fires would often start in drawers or airing cupboards and often on metal objects.

' "Jean-Pierre's wife, Annie, died after three fires broke out within seven hours at the house on 20 January; volunteer fireman Gérard David was also killed. Lab tests indicated this last fire burnt at 1300°C (2400°F) (chrome taps had melted) and witnesses claimed that the orange flames had pointed into the wind. The fatalities suffered third degree burns underneath intact clothing; the coroner said it was as if the victims had gone through a gigantic mircowave oven.

' "On 27 January, all the tiles on the roof of Madeleine Cordier's house fell off at once. Another blaze started in a wardrobe in the house of Jean-Pierre's brother, Charles, on the night of 3 February. The local magistrate said that the scientists had failed to find any 'electrical, nuclear or magnetic anomaly'. Speculations included bombardment by satellite laser beams; seismic activity releasing inflammable gas from subterranean caves; electromagnetic pollution; and 'leaking' from a 20,000 volt power line installed under the rue de Cares (scene of most of the fires) last July.

' "Vulcanologist Jean Meunier pointed out that Moirans rests on a geophysical fault line and suggested that ionised hydrogen was seeping out and igniting on contact with metal. A witch doctor from the Pyrenees said only a Vatican exorcist could save the town. However, Pascal Raffin, 35, was caught on 4 February setting fire to a child's pushchair in a garage near the house of his father, Charles, where the wardrobe had combusted the night before.

' "After two days of interrogation, young Raffin, nervous and quiet by nature, confessed to having set all the Moirans fires, but gave no reason.

' "Allegedly, he used a very slow-burning chemical next to a highly inflammable material in confined places where the oxygen was thin, delaying ignition and allowing him time to get away. He also confessed to other fires in the neighbourhood, such as the four that started within a period of four months at the barn of René Aquistapace 2 miles (3 km) away. He remained very calm during questioning and appeared detached from everything, according to a policeman. But is the case solved?

' "The explanation seems a bit too convenient for the authorities. What about those microwave-type third degree burns, reminiscent of spontaneous human combustion? We await further revelations." There you are, Ken!' 'Ta James.'[a] The *Fortean Times*'s end query is an echo of the disquiet of our toy-shop old ladies of Moirans.

[a] James is a seeker and Fortean. See his terrific in-depth interview with Robert Anton Wilson: 'Chromosome Damage!'[b] in *Fortean Times*. And like me, James corresponds with Ion Will[c] in Abidjan.

[b] Sadly, the issue in which this interview appeared (No. 79) has sold out. However, it can be obtained (along with a number of interesting *Fortean Times* extracts) through the *Fortean Times* 24-hour information fax service FortFax. Call 0891–440441 from the handset of your fax machine (handset switched to tone); after voice prompts, select document number 1046 using your fax keypad. Or phone Stracomm Ltd on 0113–2940600. For information on subscription to *Fortean Times*, phone 01373–451777 (UK, EC, World) or (516)–627–3836 (USA, Canada).

[c] Ion Will is exactly one year to the day (10 December)[1] older than me, and we went to school together, a fact not mentioned in *The Recollections of a Furtive Nudist*[2] where Ion appears as the many-armed bedsit guru. It was Ion who had the idea for the BBC Film drama I wrote some years ago, *Unfair Exchanges*, starring Julie Walters, in which I play the editor of the *Fortean Times*. I also wrote about Ion in the stage play *The Great Caper*[3] (he was played by Warren Mitchell), premiered at the Royal Court in the early seventies. Ion lives now on the Ivory Coast, married to a local beauty who heads the Abidjan Jehovah's Witness pamphlet team. Ion leaves the pamphletting to his missus, and has meanwhile risen to Chief Chicken Strangler of the Abidjan Macumba[4] Lodge. It is Ion to whom this work is dedicated. He writes a 40-or-so page letter of astoundment to me roughly every two months, usually including bizarre (too mild a word) clippings from African newspapers and mags which I forward to the *Fortean Times* (except the real cream). If they're in French, he includes his translation. So you see, he's not dead, Rose.[5]

[1] John Birt whose BBC it is (for the moment) also born same day.

[2] I felt too many links and coincidences would overtax credulity and head us into muddle.

[3] Text published in *Plays and Players* with pics of young me and nearly as young Ion and interview with us both by Michael Coveney. See pages 11 and 89 of current text.

[4] See page 91.

[5] Michael,* here's an example of how in later editions we could footnote past the stars: TRISTRAM SHANDY [trstm shdy] ¡¡†
　　* Earley.

† See note 91.**
       **Go back a few lines in the main text, Reader, or
       you'll have lost track of what it's all about.
       x Love, Ken.

22 *Reality on the Rocks* (Windfall Films for Channel 4).

23 Of the Beast?

24 The Second Treatise of the Great Seth. For details see note 16 above.

25 Di Mambro at the Pyramids in the *Paris Match*!

26 According to the Damanhur InterNet pages,[a] 'Digging inside the mountain
   is a metaphor for digging inside ourselves.'
       [a] These pages are available as follows: http://www.icom.it/user/
       damanhur//SOSTEMP.HTM. Other pages have the suffix: SO-
       SART.2HTM and SOSART1.HTM and SOSCONST.HTM and
       SOSECON.HTM and SOSYDH.HTM.

27 See 'Life Tools' page on the InterNet (p. 135 for details).

28 *PhotoReading Personal Learning Course* by Paul R. Scheele, MA
   (Learning Strategies Corporation, 900 East Wayzata Boulevard, Wayzata,
   Minnesota 55391–1836, USA).

29 See InterNet (p. 135 for details).

30 On our arrival (TV crew, Director, me), Derek Parfit picked up most of the
   crew's heavy equipment and carried it for them up to his room, *as if this
   were normal*. The crew followed, like amateur actors who didn't know
   what to do with their hands.

31 The public are shown a bit of it (plus lecturer who can't work the video)
   most Saturdays. But you MUST book. When Norman and I just showed
   up, we were told NO CHANCE. Luckily, Emma Someone was passing and
   recognised me from *Reality on the Rocks*. She said: 'You asked such
   wonderfully simple naïve questions that had been bothering most of us
   here.'

32 See John Gribbin, *Schrödinger's Kittens and the Search for Reality*
   (Phoenix, 1996, ISBN 1–85799–402–7).

33 Should Eternal Incredible have a capital 'H'? No. I hazard not. After all,
   he's nothing at all. P'raps should be written 'e and 'im and 'is. (Most likely
   SHOULDN'T BE WRITTEN ABOUT AT ALL.)

34 'Possible. Jan. 2nd 2000 we'll be told more.' Gillian. (Yes Gillian. Pity we
   can't check out with your Dad!) (Actually, that's cruel. Don't print that.)
   (Actually DO print it. Because I may be on to you, 'Gillian' – or should I
   say 'Mandy'?) (Or Birdy Ping.)

35 Damanhurians eventually take a new name of their own choosing: a plant
   and an animal. ESPERIDE I think is some kind of butterfly. When we met

her she hadn't yet come up with her second name. Now she has: ANANAS (pineapple). So her full name is Some Kind of Butterfly Pineapple. The lady who heads 'Temple Art' is Octopus Cocoa! (But it sounds sexy in the Italian.)

36 '300 tons of circuits and connections' – Damanhur Selfica InterNet page.

37 That's what they say!

38 Oberto: 'The sound of the laughter was louder than the sound of the hammers.'

39 What IS it?

40 *Illuminatus!* Adapted from the trilogy by Robert Shea and Robert Anton Wilson (Dell; ISBN 0–440–53981–1). Performed by The Science Fiction Theatre of Liverpool. Robert Anton Wilson's experience of it (and in it) is on page 223 of his excellent *Cosmic Trigger I* (New Falcon Publications, Arizona; ISBN 0–941404–46–3 / 0–56184–003–3). See also notes 21[a] and [b] above, and notes 71 and 73 below.

41 See p. 135.

42 I wanted to know what had happened to all the earth and rock and stuff that they'd bucketted out of the mountain. 'Poof!' said Oberto, with a gesture of magical vanishment. 'You poofed it away?' 'Yes!'

43 The C.W. Daniel Company Ltd, Saffron Walden; ISBN 085207–224–4. Colin Wilson is a fan of the Guirdham books. One forgets how really great Colin Wilson[a] is. I'm going to order the Complete Works from the Library and Blast 'em – Blast through the whole canon in a day!

   [a] See for example his book *Strange Powers* (Abacus / Sphere, 1975) which has an enthusiastic chapter on Arthur Guirdham, and was written as 'a postscript' to his astonishing and essential *The Occult*[1] (Mayflower Books, Granada Publishing Ltd, 1973) – 'worthy to be placed on the same shelf alongside . . . Frazer's *Golden Bough*' (Alan Hull Walton, *Books and Bookmen*).

      [1] Dedicated to Wilson's friend, author/poet Robert Graves, whose 'historical grammar of poetic myth', *The White Goddess* (Faber & Faber; ISBN 0–571–06961–4), and 1946 novel *King Jesus* (Hutchinson & Co, 1983) would sit nicely alongside your Wilson's *Occult**[*]* and Frazer's *Golden Bough*.[†]

         [*] Colin Wilson is also a favourite author of Robert Anton Wilson. See notes 21[a] and 40.

         [†] See page 57 (and notes 54 and 55).

44 *We Are One Another: Astounding evidence of group reincarnation* (C. W. Daniel (again); ISBN 0–85207–248–1). (Frontispiece: fine pic of Montségur.)

45 People who knew Arthur get upset by this Guirdham section, not because it isn't true, but because it doesn't come over what a nice man he was. (Both of them.)

46 Both comics par Gilles Chaillet Vasco, couleurs de Chantal Defachelle published by Le Lombard sur les Pays de vos Héros, Bruxelles.

47 Here, you won't believe this, but just right at that moment, as I'm going through this text putting the notes in, but right then! – just as I'm reading 'Brûlez Cathares! Brûlez!' – a plop through the letter box, and on the mat: *L'Ordre du Temple Solaire* par Renaud Marhic.[a] And listen, he dedicates the thing 'A Umberto Eco'! O! and a note. Ah! It's from Benedicte, the former French au pair (of the policeman's at No. 68) who moved into my place to look after the dogs for a couple of weeks (and help translate OC rudery) and then got run off with by the Husband of the Lady next door (Adrian, in whom I don't see the attraction). Well, let's hope they're happy. Christ! Benedicte's pregnant! Do I tell Ann? She probably knows. She's quite cheery, Ann. She's taken up jogging, but Gertie (dog) prances after her snapping at her bum. She's really nice, Ann.

> [a] Collection 'Zététique' l'Horizon Chimérique . . . Who's at the door now? Jehovah's Witness! What shall I give 'em? Parfit! They haven't had Parfit. And Minsky[1] next week.
>
> > [1] . . . actually I'll do more Parfit next week. Boggled 'em! But Minsky's book (a seeker's must) is *The Society of Mind*, a Touchstone Book, published by Simon & Schuster.

48 This is like a book catalogue . . . Par Pertuzé [who also does rude stuff] Loubatières Éditeur, 10 bis, Impasse de Saint-Simon, 31120, Portet-sur-Garonne.

49 Wait! My story is cunningly structured. You don't know what this was until near the end.

50 My outdoor snap of her, taken from the Bookshop looking up Montségur Lane, is on the back of this book. Do you know her? Reward.

51 A seeker's must is *High Weirdness by Mail. A Directory of the Fringe: Mad Prophets, Crackpots, Kooks and True Visionaries* by Rev. Ivan Stang, a Fireside Book, Simon & Schuster. You can write to all these astounding people and potty organisations. AND THEY DO REPLY. The Rev. gives tips on how best to approach each of them.

52 See 'Life, but certainly not as we know it' in *Fortean Times*, No. 86 (p. 7), May 1996.

53 I wouldn't know exactly – no watch.

54 You can get it for a quid now. Wordsworth Classics. (How did Sir James find out all that? I know someone whose uncle's got the whole thing – all twelve volumes! – and I'm going to borrow it and Blast it.)

55 For the full text look up 'Bretheren and Sisters of the Free Spirit' in the index of Sir J. G. Frazer's *The Golden Bough, A Study in Magic and Religion* (abridged, Papermac, 1995).

56 *Technicians of the Sacred*, edited with commentaries by Jerome Rothenberg (Anchor Books, 1969).

57 Michael Bradley with Deanna Theilmann-Bean, *Holy Grail Across the Atlantic: The Secret History of Canadian Discovery and Exploration* (Hounslow Press, fifth printing 1993; ISBN 0–88882–100–X).

58 And I can also tell you what it is, and do so, later.

59 *Last of the Moe Haircuts: The Influence of the Three Stooges on Twentieth-Century Culture* by Bill Flanagan, Director of the American Stooge Symposium (Contemporary Books Inc., Chicago, 1986; ISBN 0–8092–5152–3).

60 Ed Riche wrote the script for *A Secret Nation*, a movie about the cheating of the vote; and Mike Jones directed it. Paul Pope produced. Cathy Jones, Mike's sister, played the lead. It's only had one showing in the UK as far as I know, at the Edinburgh Film Festival a few years ago. Mike, Paul and Ed stayed with me before we went on to Scotland and Ed tried to get to see our relevant Governmental papers which would prove the matter one way or another. But they're not allowed to be looked at.

61 *Surviving Confederation* by F. L. Jackson (Harry Cuff Publications Ltd, St Johns, Newfoundland, 1986; ISBN 0–921191–02–2). *No Fish – And Our Lives: Some Survival Notes for Newfoundland* by Cabot Martin (Creative Publishers, St Johns, Newfoundland, 1992; ISBN 1–895387–12–4).

62 See *Infinite Jest*, David Foster Wallace's sensational read, set just after the millenium, when this (and worse) has happened. If you ever meet Wallace ask him if he knows Minsky. My guess is he does.

63 Teleported from a King's Cross lav in *The Recollections of a Furtive Nudist*. See Ken Campbell, *The Bald Trilogy* (Methuen, 1995), pp. 27, 40–5, 89, 97. Andy's doing very well these days. He lives in Toronto. He does shows quite similar to mine. I saw his last one at the Longshoremen's Protective Union Hall, and man! – it was a cracker! Mike came to it every night for its two week run there, not for the whole thing, but just for the three minutes that made him cry.

64 This and in fact several of the better phrases I found myself coming out with that night are from the best autobiography ever. (Absolutely.) Ben Hecht's *A Child of the Century* (Donald I. Fine Inc., New York; ISBN 0–917657–42–X) and in it is kinda explained why it's so unlikely to find a copy in the UK. I got mine (used) in New York.

65 I am indebted to Bryce (surname unknown) for this phrase. Bryce, a young New Zealander who had been possessed by a burning thirteenth-century Cathar in the Kensington Pizza Hut. '. . . outskirts of a village . . .

centuries ago . . . I was burning . . . in very real agony . . . others burning with me . . . and I knew the names of everyone watching . . . I knew all about everyone . . .' 'How long did this go on?' I asked, imagining twenty minutes of unrivalled antic in the Pizza Hut. 'No time,' said Bryce. 'The space between heartbeats.' I was so taken with the phrase I offered Bryce a fiver for it, which he was happy to accept.

66 Her using the phrase 'More than two' tells us something about her. If she means 'three' then she's a delightful Romancer. And I think that must be the case, because if it were four or five even, that would surely be so startling you'd merely state it?

67 Colchester Arts Centre she didn't show up at all. Reason for absence: 'Hair'. (Which is, of course, black, as affirmed.) My theory is the real reason was ferret essence.

68 See note 6 above.

69 And this was before I was into Blasting!

70 See note 21[c] above.

71 See *Illuminatus!* (op. cit.), Volume 1: The Eye in the Pyramid – has lots of stuff on Neophobes and Neophiles. See also Robert Anton Wilson's *Prometheus Rising* (New Falcon Publications, Arizona, USA; ISBN 0–941404–19–6). See notes 21[a] and [b], 40, 43* and 73.

72 A lot of this checks out. Get first *Secret and Suppressed – Banned Ideas and Hidden History* edited by Jim Keith (Feral House, PO Box 3466, Portland, OR 97208, USA; ISBN 0–922915–14–8). Also there are some addresses in the Rev. Stang's *High Weirdness by Mail* (op. cit.) – ESPECIALLY write to the guy in Finland . . . Wooo!

73 KEN: 'I haven't got them.' JAMES: 'Yes, but I have, Ken. *Communion* and *Transformation* (Arrow Books, 1988, 1989) and *Majestic* (Macdonald, 1990). Also get *Report on Communion* by Ed Conroy (Avon Books, 1990). For an entertaining and intelligent view on the abduction circus, read Jim Schnabel's *Dark White – Aliens, Abductions and the UFO Obsession* (Hamish Hamilton Ltd, 1994). And while we're at it, get Schnabel's *Round In Circles* (Penguin, 1994) on the crop circle myth – great fun and a great read. See also *Fortean Times* Nos. 82 and 83 on abductions. Also *Fortean Times* No. 86 (p. 47) for SF writer David Langford's comments on Whitley Strieber's alleged lack of a sense of humour. Robert Anton Wilson and I discuss Whitley Strieber in my interview with Wilson in *Fortean Times* No. 79:[a] "JAMES: I have often wondered whether Whitley Strieber's insistence on calling them 'visitors' rather than 'aliens' might be because of the absurdity of the notion of aliens coming half-way across the universe simply to shove probes up a horror writer's bottom. I mean, they're obviously quite a local phenomenon . . . RAW: Maybe he's got the most adorable bum in the galaxy, but somehow I doubt that." '

[a] See notes 21[a] and [b] on details of how to obtain this interview via your fax machine.

74 'I think we're fished for.' Charles Fort (from whom the *Fortean Times* takes its title).

75 I now read French books, or rather Norman reads them to me. In *Le 54ᵉ* author Thierry Huguenin refers to Solar Templar 'Marielle' – ?

76 Hawking's famous 'voice' is not his only one. At parties he twiddles his knob to a tarty Southern belle.

77 The waiter's correction is correct: Esclarimonde is Gillian's Charverknees-Strine version.

78 Apparently earliest mention of that name; known in her lifetime as 'the Angel of Rennes', in her death she was referred to as 'Ever-angel' (Evangeline).

79 What evidence for Truman's insectoidal colleagues? Norman and I are sceptical. If we meet a couple we'll go along with it. 'Til then we'll file 'em under 'dubious'. A worrying aspect is their incredibly advanced sense of humour, documented in the private papers of Gillian's father (who incidentally got a posthumous honour in Oz), which we've seen but could have been fabricated by the Gillian 'bundle' (on an old typewriter with ink-filled little 'e's and a wonky 'k'!), possibly while in trance – for a period, inspired by John Lilly,[a] she injected veterinary-intended substances into her muscles, and certainly John reports many alien encounters in that state, especially in sensory deprivation troughs.
   [a] See his book, *The Centre of the Cyclone* (Paladin Books, 1973). I interviewed John Lilly (aged eighty) for the Channel 4 Philosophers Prog – his answer to most of my questions was: 'Why don't you take K and get in a tank?'

80 Cigar and Kane Publications, Janus House, Phoenix, Arizona; ISBN 0–915179–61–X. Limited edition of 100 singed copies.

81 My caps.

82 Benedicte does it. To Adrian, a lot, I hope. When Adrian announced he was leaving his wife and children and running off with Benedicte, I said: 'But this inconveniences my dogs!' ADRIAN: 'Your dogs are not part of my consideration.'

83 Mrs D serves a kind of slimy oriental gruyère known locally as Holy Grail – because it makes you feel funny.

84 Round about where Paul Pope (!) (see note 60) and Liza now live. Paul's going to stick a plaque up about it all when he's got a moment.

85 Tea or Wha'?'s Mum and Dad thought Christopher was a smasher – and he had a NEWFOUNDLANDER'S TIME for the little brothers. He was introduced as a genuine Newf – in fact he's originally from Halifax, but there arose no problem with that. Dad has allowed him to purchase his daughter on a carefully worked-out instalment plan. A Live (with 'er) Now Pay Later deal. Dad's going to go over and help set the Caff kitchens up.

He speaks little English, but with time and mime, Christopher has made real contact and impressed Mr Vuong with his knowledge of the early career of Chuck Norris. They often sit up late together watching videos by and about Bruce Lee and Jackie Chan in original Chinese.

86 See note 21[b] for subscription details and fax novelties.

87 If her Mum does come to the wedding in St Johns, and presumably has to sit through this first, I'm going to get her up and show them. It's an area of Humour neglected in the West – even (so far as I'm aware) in Newfoundland.

88 Mrs D's establishment ('The Montségur Fotedor'?) worth visiting for the seating arrangement alone – not of the Caff – but of the proprietress, she having had her personal 'seat' dusted ready, expectant and upholstered for a SELF, and Oberto's instruction of how to astound one onto it. The 'in' crowd always greet Mrs D with "Ow's yer SELF, then?'

89 And, yes, data is coming in. I've now got round to reading my Milton William Cooper's *Behold a Pale Horse* Light Technology Publishing, PO Box 1495, Sedona, AZ 86336, (ISBN 0–929385–22–5), and on page 72 I find Tea or Wha'?'s spiraggle doodles all round the bit about the spacecraft Galileo with its payload of 49.7 pounds of plutonium and plan to blast Jupiter apart. I think 'Gillian' may have been a splendid hoax. Some friend of Pud's. And they'd put together 'Gillian' for me. (A low, disguised, but Striney female voice left on my answermachine saying only: 'Just wanted to find out what kind of wanker you are.') Suggestion in BBC Club Bar, when I described Gillian, that it may have been a Mandy Chin (or Chang?) who had something to do with poetry programming on *Arena* and is back in Oz at the moment? Tiddley Pud denies it. But that means little. But girls! So well done! Gillian! Mandy? (BBC Chap suggests I may have been an innocent way of passing Mandy's time while her husband was away.) Anyway – Brilliant! (Another theory is it was a Birdy Ping, half Burmese Oz, who used to inject herself with Ketamine and wallow in dingey troughs with J. Lilly in Hawaii.) But Gillian – Mandy – Birdy – please come by and sign your hoax! – But if that was all rot how did Norman come in? Norman had been knocking for years – since 1949 at least. Who is pulling whose strings? Where is the end of a Line of Synchronos?

90 Stop Press June 17th. Thieu-Hoa says that now she's a Grade Three citizen (one of the 'Sacred People' of the Nation of Damanhur) and going to live until seventy or more, she isn't going to marry Christopher – not on the show, and not yet anyway: marrying him was the sort of thing you did if you only had life-expectancy of thirty-five years. Now – well, life would INCLUDE the Arctic Café and with Christopher (but fear, you see, lest marriage somehow fucked up their terrific relationship . . . her thing with Christopher was BIGGER than marriage and therefore shouldn't be put at risk by marrying). Christopher didn't mind because since Damanhur she was so 'nice'. Ed (on phone) says she can't get away with that – 'We'll call her Mrs Darlington anyway and we won't go to the place unless it's called "Mrs Darlington's Musical Café" and if anyone asks why, we'll book

you, Ken, to come and tell us again.' Ed says Cathy's now got bouncing baby daughter and hinting she's going to legitimise the whole thing by marrying the non-drinking Drinking Buddhist from Halifax. If you're likely short of a wedding for your show, ring Cathy (Ed's tip). (I have; she's thinking about it . . .) A judge (met in the Ship Inn) had been lined up to officiate and he wants to come anyway but he *would* like to marry someone during concert if at all possible. I'd marry the Lady from Montségur for them if I knew who or where she was, or Mandy Chin-Chang. Or Birdy Ping (where are you, girls?). Anything, rather than disappoint my Newf seekers. Thieu-Hoa says, before she can marry a more important 'marriage' must take place: the marriage of Newfoundland and Damanhur . . . her commission, to get the two great Secret Nations to unite. On Oberto's World Map, the Lines of Synchronos don't yet reach to St Johns . . . By her synchronistic manipulations, she assures me, they will. These things achieved, and Christopher still shaping up, she'll marry him then, maybe.

91 These footnotes have given me an idea, Michael[a] . . . Maybe that ISN'T the end – if this book sells really well (and I think it'll be big back home), we could keep bringing out new editions which double in size each time, with footnotes of footnotes of footnotes stretching through TIME, PLACE AND DIMENSIONS, becoming eventually a monstrous selfcatious spiraggle – the Line of Synchronos reaching out to the stars and far beyond – full of sound and fury and signifying Gnothing.[b]

   [a] Michael Earley. Publisher, Methuen.

   [b] I mean there's loads more on Benedicte . . .

SEEKERS: For more information see the InterNet web page 'Tinkers in the net' (http://www.tinkers.co.uk).